COMMUNITY YOUTH CLUB HANDBOOK

Everything you need to know to start a youth club!

Kirstie Brown and Jeff Brown

COMMUNITY YOUTH CLUB HANDBOOK

Everything you need to know to start a youth club!

Kirstie Brown and Jeff Brown

Copyright © 2013

ISBN: 978-0-9060890-1-9

Published by Somerset County Council in conjunction with Writersworld, this book is produced entirely in the UK, is available to order from most book shops in the United Kingdom, and is also globally available via UK-based Internet book retailers.

Copy edited by Ian Large

Cover design by Jag Lall

WRITERSWORLD
2 Bear Close Flats
Bear Close
Woodstock
Oxfordshire
OX20 1JX
United Kingdom
Telephone: 0044 (0)1993 812500

www.writersworld.co.uk

The text pages of this book are produced via an independent certification process that ensures the trees from which the paper is produced come from well managed sources that exclude the risk of using illegally logged timber while leaving options to use post-consumer recycled paper as well.

Dedication and disclaimer

This is book is dedicated to the hundreds of young people and staff we've worked with over the years and who have provided us the opportunities and experience necessary to write it. Thanks also to all the staff at Somerset Youth and Community Service who have made suggestions and amendments to the text along the way. Whilst their advice has been invaluable, any mistakes are all our own.

We believe this book's content is original work, but acknowledge it has been influenced by a range of written and oral sources over the years. If you think we've infringed the copyright of another author please let us know. We'll happily set the record straight and amend future editions.

Although the authors and publisher have made every effort to ensure that the information in this book was correct at the time of publication, the authors and publisher do not assume and hereby disclaim any liability to any party for any loss, damage, or disruption caused by errors or omissions, whether such errors or omissions result from negligence, accident, or any other cause.

Contents

Contents

Appendices

Contents

Contents

Contents

1. Introduction

Many young people complain that there isn't enough to do and many adults are concerned that young people with nowhere to go and nothing to do will cause or get into trouble. One solution is to set up a youth club or project. Offering young people an informal environment where they can spend time and take part in activities can create a sense of belonging and provide them with an opportunity to take responsibility for themselves and the club, and have influence in their community. Adults involved in the club become role models and help promote respect and understanding between the generations as well as providing support and a listening ear to young people when they need it. Young people pick up the values of the club, possibly including a spirit of volunteering, and as they get older they may choose to take on an active leadership role.

1.1 Why this handbook?

Increasingly, youth clubs and other projects for young people are run by volunteers and small community-based organisations. This handbook is aimed at helping you through the process of starting a voluntary youth club in Somerset. Much of the information is relevant to a youth club anywhere in the UK, but some is specific to Somerset.

1.2 About this handbook

Starting a youth club can seem very complicated and difficult. We've broken it down into a series of steps, and explained each of these and how they fit into the overall process. We've also provided templates and examples of forms, policies and other paperwork which you can use and edit to create the documents that you need for your club or project.

The sections are:

- **First thoughts**
  This section is about working out what you are trying to achieve, identifying if there's a need for a youth project and understanding the differences between delivering youth work and the governance that needs to be in place to manage it well and safely.

- **The management committee**
  This section explores legal status, committee roles and responsibilities and the meetings that might be held.

- **Money matters**
  This looks at managing and raising money.

- **Policies and paperwork**
  This section looks at the policies you must have and could have, as well as outlining the types of paperwork it's useful to have, including a word on consent forms.

- **Insurance**
  Explores the insurance that youth clubs must have and may have.

- **Health and safety in youth work**
  This section looks at what you need to think about and do to ensure that your youth work activities are safe for young people and staff.

- **Managing paid and unpaid staff**
  This includes the recruitment process, holding staff meetings, supervising staff, tax and payroll, record keeping and using self-employed staff and contractors.

- **Outsourcing your youth work**
  This covers the pros and cons of outsourcing and how to go about it.

- **Building management**
  This section explores how to safely run a public building, the issues involved in hiring your building out and things to be aware of if you are hiring building space from another organisation.

- **Running your youth club**
  This section looks at what you want to achieve with your youth club, running the sessions, getting young people to attend, public relations, programme planning, supervising behaviour, trips, activities and what to do if things go wrong.

- **From positive activities to youth work**
  If you're running a drop-in youth club and want to develop into a club providing a programme of developmental activities, this is the section to read.

- **Involving young people in decision making and volunteering**
  This looks at how to start giving young people more responsibility in their club and their communities.

- **Ensuring Quality**
  This section looks at what you need to look out for to ensure that the youth club is being well run and providing a good service for young people.

1. Introduction

- **Support from Somerset County Council and other organisations**
  This last section outlines the help and support that is available from SCC and other organisations across the county.

- **Appendices**
  This section contains a wide range of sample documents that have been referred to in the previous sections.

1.3 How to use this handbook

If you're starting from scratch, it is probably best to read this handbook from start to finish, referring to the appendices as they are referenced in the text. If you've already started your youth club, it's best to dip into the things you want to know about.

1.4 Disclaimer

This publication gives general guidance and good practice advice only and should not be regarded as a complete or authoritative statement of the law.

If you wish to check the exact legal position in relation to any aspect of setting up your youth club, you should seek your own legal advice.

We have done our best to ensure that the web links are relevant and appropriate, but are not responsible for non-Somerset County Council web content.

This handbook is the result of many years of youth work practice. Some of the appendices may originally have been sourced from other organisations, the origins of which are now lost. If you think that anything in this book has not been properly acknowledged, or should not be included, please let us know and we will do our best to rectify the situation. We would welcome any comments or feedback that you have about this handbook. Please contact youthservice@somerset.gov.uk or telephone 01823 349852.

2. First thoughts

Before you set up your youth club, you need to be clear about what you are trying to achieve, so that you can measure your progress.

2.1 What are you trying to achieve?

Are you aiming to:

- Set up a drop-in for young people to come and go as they like, which is warm and dry and has refreshments available?
- Set up a youth club, which is also warm and dry, but has a tuck shop and an organised programme with fun activities that are aimed at encouraging young people to spend the whole evening with you?
- Set up a youth club with all of the above, staff that are happy to give information and advice and that provides educational activities aimed at developing young people's skills, knowledge and potential?
- Set up a youth club with all the above which aims to get young people to help with the running and also encourages them to take more of a part in community matters, such as having a voice on the town or parish council or taking part in community activities, such as a Remembrance Day Parade or the local fete?

The first two are often referred to as a 'positive activity', the last two as 'youth work'. As you can see, what you're aiming to do can have a big impact on what you need to plan for. For example, you need fewer staff for a busy drop-in than a busy youth club – because staff have activities to run, rather than just an area to supervise.

2.2 How do you know there's a need for a youth club?

Before starting to organise your youth club, you need to check that it is what young people want. Anecdotal reports are not enough! The best thing to do is to go out in the area and ask the young people you meet what they think – don't forget to explain who you are and why you want to know! The key questions are:

- If we set up a youth club, would you and your mates go?
- What would you like to do there?
- How far would you travel to get there?
- What nights would you prefer to go?
- How much would you be willing to pay to get in?
- Would you be willing to help out with the youth club? How?

It's also useful to keep a track of the age and gender of the young people you talk to, so that you know who is likely to come to the club.

Always make sure you tell the young people (afterwards) what you may be able to do as you could otherwise set up unrealistic expectations. The other bonus of doing this kind of research is that you might be able to recruit some young people to help you make decisions about the youth club and do some of the work around setting it up.

If you decide to go out on the streets, don't go alone and always have some ID with you. Young people can be very suspicious of strangers and they have a right to know who you are and why you are approaching them. Check out your route first, don't go anywhere that will put you in danger and let the local police know what you're doing. Go out during school holidays, at weekends or evenings – but always make sure you're safe.

If walking the streets is a step too far for you, you could try talking to the local school to see if you can speak to young people there or send in a questionnaire. Alternatively, you could talk to adults who run local hobby clubs and see if they have any young people attending – you can then see if they don't mind you coming along to talk to the young people there. Sports, arts and drama groups commonly have young people attending.

2.3 The governance/delivery split

It is worth thinking about, and being clear about, the different roles of people who are helping you set up your youth club. There are two main areas of responsibility:

- **Governance** ensuring that the club has enough funding, the right policies and is properly organised
- **Delivery** the adults who staff the sessions and are responsible for providing things for the young people to do

Volunteers usually do a bit of both, but it is worth being clear what is expected of them and ensuring they understand that they don't have to do both if they don't want to. Some people are great at organising, but not so good at dealing with teenagers, others are great with teenagers but couldn't organise a thing. There is room for both types when running a youth club. It's a good idea to start with a volunteer's strengths and then help them develop any skills they feel they need. It is important that at least one person who runs the youth club sessions attends management meetings, but this is to ensure that young people's views are put forward and the managers of the club know what's going on, rather than anything else.

Governance includes:

- The legal status of the organisation and its constitution
- Setting the aim and objectives of the organisation
- Managing the money
- Arranging the correct insurances
- Adopting the appropriate policies for the club
- Finding and negotiating the use of a suitable venue
- Ensuring the proper health and safety measures are in place
- Managing paid staff and volunteers and making sure they're properly trained
- Fundraising and reporting to funders
- Making sure the community knows what's happening and is supportive (this includes marketing and publicity of the club – which is best done with young people)

Delivery includes:

- Opening when the club says it will open
- Equipment being out, checked and ready to use
- Clear ground rules for behaviour at the club that the young people know about and have agreed to
- Being respectful to young people
- Making sure all equipment and activities are safe for young people
- A planned programme (if you're having one) for young people to take part in
- A stocked coffee bar (if you're having one)

This handbook is mainly focussed on managing and running youth clubs and what is needed to ensure that clubs are run legally and safely. For more information about working directly with young people and how to do it well, please see **Section 15** '**Support from Somerset County Council and other organisations**' for a list of organisations that may be able to help you.

2. First thoughts

3. The management committee

It's easier to manage a youth club with a team of people – it's a lot of work for just one or two people. This team is usually called a management committee and it has a legal status.

3.1 Legal status

In the eyes of the law, an organisation is either:

- a collection of individuals working together – an unincorporated association, or
- a body with a separate existence from the individuals belonging to it – a corporate body such as a limited company

Most voluntary organisations begin as unincorporated organisations, and stay that way, particularly if they are small. A group of people can form one cheaply and simply; by agreeing some basic rules and policies, and writing these down, so that everyone is clear about the aims of the organisation, what it will do and how it will be managed. This is what youth club management committees usually are.

The law views an unincorporated organisation as a collection of individuals, which means it cannot own property, enter into contracts or take part in a lawsuit in its own right. Its officers and committee members have to do these things as individuals.

If an unincorporated organisation ends up by owing money, the members can be personally liable to meet any debts from their own pockets. This is called unlimited liability, and shows the importance of ensuring the organisation has the right insurance and is well-managed!

If your organisation grows you may consider becoming a registered charity. This status brings some benefits in relation to tax, fundraising and liability protection, but requires a much greater level of governance and financial reporting, so is more expensive and time consuming. To consider registered charity status an organisation currently needs a minimum of £5,000 per year income, and this is more than many small voluntary youth clubs. For most small voluntary organisations, the cost and complexity of being a registered charity probably outweigh the benefits. It is impossible to state here the point where an organisation should convert, so as you grow and you want to provide a larger, more professional service, you should take advice about the pros and cons of charitable status. More information is available on the Charity Commission website www.charitycommission.gov.uk.

3.2 Committee responsibilities

Any organisation needs to ensure it is well-run and does what it is trying to do – this is called governance. In large companies governance is the responsibility of the board of directors, in smaller voluntary groups it is done by the management committee.

Governance includes:

- The legal status of the organisation and its constitution
- Setting the aim and objectives of the organisation
- Managing the money
- Arranging the correct insurances
- Adopting the appropriate policies for the club
- Finding and negotiating the use of a suitable venue
- Ensuring the proper health and safety measures are in place
- Managing paid staff/volunteers and making sure they're properly trained
- Fundraising and reporting to funders
- Making sure the community knows what's happening and is supportive (this includes marketing and publicity of the club – which is best done with young people)

The founding document for the club is its constitution. This lays out what the club is trying to achieve, who for, and how. Sample constitutions are included in **Appendix 4**. Pick the one that best suits your club, make whatever amendments are required and agree it at an early committee meeting.

3.3 Committee roles

As a minimum, the committee should have a chairperson, secretary and treasurer. Your committee could also have a president, vice-chairperson, club leader, young people's representatives, committee members, co-opted members and ex-officio members.

All members should be elected at the Annual General Meeting (AGM) as set out in your constitution.

General outlines of the responsibilities of these roles are listed below:

- **President**

This is often an 'honorary' role given to a local celebrity whose involvement can help bring publicity and money to the club. This role

SOMERSET County Council

3. Management committee

is more of a figurehead who gives awards and prizes and generally does public relations for the club. They also chair the AGM and act as an adviser. Other than this, they have the role of an ordinary committee member (see below).

- **Chairperson**

The chairperson needs to have the energy to make the club happen and keep it going. The chairperson ensures that the club keeps on track by doing what it sets out to do and also making sure that others on the committee do what they've said they'll do. S/he chairs meetings, consults on and then sets the agenda and ensures that the club has adequate policies and insurances. They are also responsible for ensuring that the club's health and safety responsibilities are met. The chairperson also usually supervises the staff member in charge, ensures that recruitment and vetting is properly done and produces the annual report for the AGM.

The chairperson also generally represents the committee on any other groups, ensures regular contact with the youth club (usually through the youth club staff member in charge) and also visits the club and the youth club members' committee (if there is one). The chairperson can delegate any of these responsibilities to other committee members (usually to a vice-chairperson) but is responsible for ensuring that this work is done.

- **Vice-chairperson**

The vice-chairperson deputises for the chairperson when necessary and may take on any of the responsibilities mentioned above, on behalf of the chairperson.

- **Treasurer**

The treasurer needs to be honest, reliable and good with figures. Their main role is to keep the accounts up to date and in good order, to bank any monies received and be the financial adviser to the committee, particularly in relation to whether or not the club can afford to do a project, pay its staff and its bills. The treasurer prepares a report for the management committee meetings and the AGM, which s/he attends. The treasurer is also responsible for preparing accounts for scrutiny/auditing as required by the constitution.

- **Secretary**

The secretary needs to be organised, a good communicator and be prepared to keep records and paperwork up to date. S/he prepares and distributes the paperwork for committee meetings, takes minutes at the committee and any other meetings. Timescales etc for this are usually detailed in the constitution.

- **Young people's representatives**

These are young people who attend the club and represent the views of the young people who attend the club (not just their own views).

They also report back to club members about what the management committee views are, and advise on what young people will think of club policy and any other decision making. Young people's representatives are essential as they are the experts on being young people. It's a good idea to have a minimum of two young people and to give them some basic training and background information before they start. You could have a young people's sub-committee that reports to the main committee. This would allow greater access to decision making for young people attending the club and be a less formal or scary option for more young people to take part in. See **Section 13 'Involving young people in decision making and volunteering'** for more information on young people's members' groups.

- **Club leader**

This is usually the staff member in charge of the youth club sessions. They attend meetings and present a report about the activities of the club, the achievements of young people and any issues that they feel the management committee need to consider. They also support the participation of the young people's representatives.

- **Committee members**

These are usually members of the community with an interest in helping the youth club. Their role is similar to that of the young people's representatives, but with a community focus. They sometimes have a special interest area and so are keen to help on club projects.

- **Co-opted members**

These are members who are not elected, but asked to join the committee. This could be because they have an area of expertise, they're representing interested groups in the community, they are representing groups who use the building or they want to join before the next committee election at the AGM. They may have voting rights. The types of people who can join and whether or not they have voting rights needs to be set out in your constitution.

- **Ex-officio members**

These are committee members who provide specialist input – such as administrators, building managers or local authority youth work managers – who advise the committee but do not have voting rights. Again, the types of people who can join needs to be set out in your constitution.

All management committee members help out with projects and the work of the committee, as well as advising on and helping to set club policy. It is a good idea to have all adult members DBS cleared, as they are likely to come into contact with young people in their official management committee capacity.

SOMERSET
County Council

3. Management committee

3. Management committee

As well as the responsibilities above, there are a number of other functions that the committee carries out, but these don't have to be the responsibility of one person. As long as you know who is doing what, and they are doing it, these can be shared:

- Publicity – promoting the club, recruiting young people
- Fundraising – either an ongoing process to help with general costs or specifically for an activity or piece of equipment
- Maintaining the building
- Taking bookings
- Supporting volunteers.
- Liaising with other clubs
- Other responsibilities specific to the club

3.4 Committee membership

Committee members need to support what the club is trying to do, and have the time to carry out their role. It is helpful to get a cross-section of age groups on the committee, and if there are people in the community with specialist skills (finance, fundraising, etc.) that can be used, so much the better. It is vital that the committee hears young people's voices, so we recommend you aim for at least two club members on the committee. It may take time to get to this position (as young people may need tempting into it, or training), so a member of staff should ensure that young people's needs, views and aspirations are taken into account when the committee makes decisions.

It is worth noting that occasionally the committee may have to make a decision that is unpopular with young people or the staff that run the club, but is the right thing to do. This could be around cancelling a planned activity because there isn't enough money, changing the opening hours because there are too few staff, or challenging a member of staff who has done something they shouldn't have.

In this situation it is important that the right decision can be made, and it is recommended that the committee should, therefore, have more members who don't run the club than those that do.

3.5 Youth club meetings

It is important to have regular meetings so that communication takes place and things can be resolved or moved forward. The following are the sorts of meetings that youth clubs generally have as part of their management. All meetings should have minutes and, if possible, a clear task list sent out to members.

- **Management committee meetings**
The frequency of management committee meetings is set out in the constitution, but they are usually between four and six times a year.

They are attended by all members (including young people's representatives) and deal with the business of running the club. A sample agenda could include:

1. Welcome
2. Apologies
3. Minutes of the last meeting
4. Matters arising and outstanding actions
5. Staff Member in Charge of the club's update (usually supported by a written report)
6. Club member update
7. Financial information and fundraising
8. Building matters
9. Specific projects or business (for example, repainting the basketball court, the community fun day or setting up a members' group)
10. Any other business
11. Date of next meeting

- **Annual General Meeting (AGM)**

This will take place once a year and is a time to sum up the previous year and plan for the future. It is also the place where committee members are elected (or re-elected). The AGM is a public meeting and so parents and other interested parties can attend and should be invited. The timing and communication about the AGM is set out in the constitution. All members should attend. A sample AGM agenda could include:

1. Welcome
2. Apologies
3. Minutes of the last AGM
4. Matters arising
5. Chairperson's report
6. Staff member in charge of the club's report
7. Treasurer's report
8. Members' group report
9. Election of officers:
   a. President
   b. Chair
   c. Vice-chair
   d. Treasurer
   e. Secretary
10. Election of committee members
11. Any other business
12. Date of next meeting

As these are pubic meetings, it's nice to have refreshments and nibbles before and afterwards, so that people have time to chat and network.

3. Management committee

- **Members' groups' meetings**

Please see **Section 13 'Involving young people in decision making and volunteering'** for more information on young people's members' groups.

- **Project sub-committees**

These are usually made up of members of the management committee, sometimes with outsiders to help, and are 'job and finish' groups. They report to the management committee and have a specific remit (usually given to them by the management committee) and disband when they've finished their task. Examples could include:

- Looking at different ways of fundraising
- Setting up a youth parish council
- Organising a community fun day
- Anything else that needs specific work to take it forward

It's always good to have at least one young person on any of these groups.

- **Staff meetings**

Usually run by the staff member in charge, these are meetings when all staff (paid or unpaid) meet to discuss the programme of the club, any issues with young people, any projects that are being undertaken and get and give information on the club itself.

3.6 And finally...

The key to running an efficient management committee is organisation and clarity.

- Be clear about what you want the youth club to achieve
- Be clear about the management structure needed to achieve it
- Make sure people understand the roles they've taken on
- Don't wear people out with constant meetings
- Make sure meetings have a clear task
- Make sure minutes are circulated, tasks allocated and followed up and the progress that you make is known by all

You don't want your committee, or any other of your volunteers, getting meeting fatigue!

It is worth remembering that volunteers are committing their own, free time, to make the youth club work. Try to minimise any extra time that they need to put into tasks they might not have volunteered to do. Volunteers can burn out too!

4. Money matters

No matter how many volunteers you have, the club won't survive without money – you'll spend it and receive it. There are many things that you'll spend money on. These may include:

- Renting a venue for the club *or*
- Building repair and maintenance (if you own it)
- Buying or renting equipment for young people to use
- Insurances and affiliation to groups that can provide help
- Food and drink for the coffee bar or tuck shop
- Minibus rental for trips and visits
- Tickets and entry to events and activities for young people
- Caretaking and cleaning (labour and materials)
- Communication (postage, website)
- Repairing damages (accidents do happen, no matter how careful everyone is)
- Licences (TV, music playing etc.)
- Health and safety (fire extinguisher inspection, portable appliance testing)
- Staff expenses (salaries, training, travel)

The ways you'll generate income will probably include:

- Subscriptions from young people each time they attend the club
- Donations from local people who want to support the club
- Grants from charitable sources in response to specific requests
- Money raised through events and campaigns
- Charging young people for events you take them to
- Profit from the coffee bar or tuck shop
- Renting your building out to other users (if you have a building)

It is vital that any money the club has is managed and accounted for properly – for this you need a treasurer.

4.1 Treasurer's role and responsibilities

The treasurer is ultimately responsible for ensuring that the finances of the club are organised and managed effectively through a specific and separate club bank account.

The treasurer manages all income, including:

- Collecting subscriptions and money owed to the club

- Ensuring that income is promptly paid into the bank or building society
- Recording information about all money received and issuing receipts

The treasurer manages all expenditure, including:

- Paying the bills and recording the information

The treasurer manages legal requirements, including:

- Dealing with the payroll and income tax for paid employees
- Helping to prepare and submit documents required by law (e.g. VAT returns, PAYE and National Insurance returns and tax returns) and those required by grant aid and funding agreements

The treasurer also:

- Keeps up-to-date records of all financial transactions
- Reports regularly to the committee on the club's financial status
- Identifies fundraising opportunities (e.g. grant programmes)
- Arranges for the accounts to be audited
- Prepares year-end accounts to present to the auditor
- Presents a financial report to the Annual General Meeting (AGM)
- Deals with financial planning, including producing an annual budget and monitoring it throughout the year

Some of these duties can be delegated to a professional (accountant, fundraiser etc), but the treasurer is still ultimately responsible. It is up to the treasurer to make sure any delegated work is carried out correctly.

To be effective, the treasurer must have:

- Adequate time to perform the role
- Enthusiasm, honesty and integrity
- Good communication and organisational skills
- The ability to keep records and an eye for detail
- Confidence with numbers and the ability to handle money carefully
- An understanding of basic bookkeeping and the facilities to carry out the role (e.g. laptop or accounts book, receipt book, chequebook and somewhere to keep the records securely)

There are many computer packages on the market dedicated to basic accountancy and bookkeeping. For larger clubs these may be worth the investment, otherwise a spreadsheet or cashbook will do

the job. Good stationery shops sell cashbooks designed to help you keep the necessary records as well as 'how to' guides to basic bookkeeping and accounts.

For very keen or very new treasurers, many local colleges run basic bookkeeping and accountancy evening courses, which can help you gain the necessary skills.

This is also a good opportunity for a young person to develop skills and understanding as 'shadow' treasurer, to learn the ropes and have a role in helping run the club.

For more detailed information about accounting requirements, talk to an accountant.

4.2 Subscriptions and donations

All income must be treated in the same way – recorded and banked as soon as possible.

- Young people's subscriptions should be recorded on the session sheet and added up at the end. You must give someone a receipt for their money if they want one, so while it is rare to give a young person a receipt for their weekly subs, you should have a receipt book handy in case they ask. Always use a receipt book that includes a duplicate so that you have a good record.

- Money for trips and visits should be recorded separately from subs so you can see how much you have, and your records should show the young person's name. Always give a receipt for this type of income, so you have a duplicate record in case there's a question about how much a young person has paid.

- Coffee bar income should be clearly recorded so you can see whether the coffee bar covers its costs or makes a profit. Again, it's unlikely you'll have to give a young person a receipt for sweets and drinks, but you must do if they ask.

- Some donations come with strings and some don't. You must know what the money was donated for, so keeping accurate records is important. You must be able to give a receipt for a donation, and if it's for a specific purpose (e.g. repairing the roof or supporting the summer activity programme) then the receipt should include this information. The club's account records must show these donations as 'restricted funds' until they're spent and the end of year statement of accounts should note how restricted funds were spent.

4. Money matters

4. Money matters

4.3 VAT

VAT is a tax that's charged on most business transactions. Businesses add VAT to the price they charge when they provide goods and services to:

- Business customers – for example a clothing manufacturer adds VAT to the prices they charge a clothes shop
- Non-business customers – members of the public or 'consumers' – for example a hairdresser includes VAT in the prices they charge members of the public

If you're a VAT-registered business, in most cases you:

- Charge VAT on the goods and services you provide
- Reclaim the VAT you pay when you buy goods and services for your business

The turnover threshold above which organisations must register for VAT is currently £77,000 per year. If your turnover is below that, you don't need to register. Registered groups can claim back the VAT they pay when purchasing goods and services, but for small youth groups it's rarely worth the extra work.

More detailed information about VAT can be found on the HM Revenue and Customs website (www.hmrc.gov.uk) or you can talk to an accountant, who will advise whether you should consider registration.

4.4 PAYE and tax

When you take on a new employee there are important checks you'll have to make. You'll need to decide what their correct employment status is and also check they can legally work for you. If you then employ them, you'll need to consider whether you should operate PAYE (Pay As You Earn) on their earnings. If you have an accountant or someone with payroll experience on the committee they can probably help. Otherwise, refer to the HM Revenue and Customs website (www.hmrc.gov.uk) or New Employer helpline (0845 6070143) for more information.

It's your responsibility to decide on the correct employment status of someone who works for you. If you get their employment status wrong you might have to pay extra tax, National Insurance contributions, interest and a penalty.

This means that you've got to decide whether they're an employee or self-employed. You can't simply accept that someone's self-

employed because they say they are. A person's employment status depends on the terms of the contract between you:

- a contract of service usually makes them an employee
- a contract for services usually makes them self-employed

HM Revenue & Customs' guide *Employment status: employed or self-employed?* will help you decide what sort of contract it is and explains what you have to take into account to make your decision. Search for this on www.hmrc.gov.uk.

4.5 Payroll services

Where a club doesn't have its own payroll system this can be dealt with through a payroll bureau. The services available vary and it is worth spending time to make sure you find a supplier that can meet your needs. Information about suppliers that can help small youth groups is provided in **Appendix 47**.

4.6 Fundraising

Very few clubs can survive on the income they get from young people, and most need to find money from other places to help sustain the club.

Fundraising is the art of getting money – for specific projects, club activities or sometimes just to pay the rent. There are many ways of raising money, including:

- Membership subscriptions
- Seeking donations
- Applying for grants
- Organising fund-raising events and activities
- Obtaining sponsorship

Before you think about raising money you should consider:

- How much money you currently have
- What you want money for
- How much extra money you need
- What the best way of raising funds is

The person responsible for fundraising (possibly the Treasurer) should know:

- What makes the club worthy of support
- How to tell people about the value of the club

- How to identify people and organisations that might help
- How to reach these potential supporters
- How to get a quick and helpful response

The things in the club that need extra funding must be agreed to help you work out how much money you need and what methods will be best to raise it. For example, if you need sports equipment, a raffle or small local event would probably raise enough money. On the other hand, if you want a new minibus your target is much larger and likely to require more substantial sponsorship or a grant.

It is a good idea to involve young people in all your fundraising (make sure you have parental consent) – whether it's helping run a car boot sale or writing a large funding bid. You must also make sure you're raising money for things young people want, so you'll need to consult them – most funders will ask about this, and there's no point in buying something that young people won't use.

Fundraising activities are only limited by your imagination and the facilities you have. Not all these suggestions will be possible, but it's a good starting point.

Social events:

- Bowling or skittles evening – contact your local pub landlord and ask
- Breakfast morning – bacon sandwiches all round!
- Coffee morning – ask the village hall committee
- Concert or disco – in the pub or village hall
- Quiz or race night
- Talent or fashion show – great for involving young people
- Themed party – Halloween, Easter, murder mystery evenings etc.
- Barbeques
- Charity matches (involving local teams)

Sponsored activities:

- Giving up chocolate, sweets, fizzy drinks, using Facebook
- Growing, shaving or waxing moustaches, beards, or hairy legs – involve the committee and volunteers
- Marathon game, dance or juggle
- One-day fast
- Pram push or wheelbarrow race
- Record-breaking attempts – also good for publicity
- Swim, walk, run, hop, three-legged run, cycle – involve adults and young people

Other events:

- Auction of items or promises, raffle or tombola
- Bring-and-buy, car boot or jumble sale
- Collections at local events (for example, fun days or carnivals – always ask permission of the organisers)
- Car wash
- Donations in lieu of gifts for birthdays, weddings and anniversaries

If you can find sources of regular income it makes fundraising easier. This may be possible through grant aid or donations. Approach the parish or town council to find out if they'll commit to giving the club money each year. They may not agree more than one year at a time, but once you've shown the benefit of the club it makes future years' applications more likely to succeed.

Some clubs have a Vice-Presidents' scheme, where people who donate an agreed amount (often £50 or £100) each year are invited to visit the club, asked to present certificates, judge competitions, and are publicly thanked at the club's AGM. You can also include their names on the club notice board and headed paper if there's room. This is a useful way to keep contact with people who are well-respected in the community and can often help with publicity and access to other helpful people and information.

Other clubs have found regular sponsors from businesses in their communities – these can be listed (with thanks) in newsletters and on the notice board in the club itself.

4.7 Grant aid

Sources of grant aid come and go as funding organisations review and update their priorities, but there are some which remain fairly constant. These include:

The Big Lottery Fund	www.biglotteryfund.org.uk
Comic Relief	www.comicrelief.com
BBC Children in Need	www.bbc.co.uk/pudsey
Sport Relief	www.sportrelief.com
Somerset Community Foundation	www.somersetcf.org.uk

There are many online packages that help you find funding, but you often have to register (and pay) to use the service. Your local volunteer bureau or the Council for Voluntary Service (CVS) probably has a subscription and will help you use the service. The main ones are:

4. Money matters

South Somerset Volunteer and Community Association
www.ssvca.org.uk

Mendip and Sedgemoor Community Support
www.mendipcommunitysupport.org.uk

Taunton Volunteer Action
www.tauntonva.org.uk

Engage West Somerset
www.engagews.org.uk

There are many grant programmes and charitable trusts dedicated to supporting causes in a specific area or addressing a specific need. Most of these can be found via the online packages noted above, or through local knowledge. Local knowledge is available through:

Somerset Youth & Community Service
www.somersetyouth.co.uk

Somerset Rural Youth Project
www.sryp.org.uk

Children & Young People's Partnership
www.chypps.org.uk

Contact your parish or town council to find out what grant aid they can provide, and your district council can often advise on funding to support sports and arts activities.

A few minutes searching the internet will generally provide a number of potential places to either apply for funding or to get more detailed information about what is available. Please also see **Appendix 8**, which lists other sources of funding for youth work.

5. Policies and paperwork

This section deals with the policies and paperwork that need to be in place when running a youth club. Some of it is 'nice to do' and some of it is 'must do'. Which is which will be clearly labelled. Any club policies must be adopted by the management committee and staff need to know what they are.

5.1 Mandatory policies

Your youth club **must have** the following policies in place:

- **Child protection (or safeguarding) policy**
This sets out how you will try to protect young people from abuse when they use your youth club. A sample policy can be seen in **Appendix 2**.

- **Staff vetting policy**
This sets out how you will check whether or not adults staffing your youth club are suitable to work with young people. Whilst it is not a legal requirement to have all staff (paid or voluntary) checked through the Disclosure and Barring Service (DBS, previously the CRB), it is good practice. When the DBS receives an application they check the person's details against the relevant national databases to confirm whether or not it's appropriate for that person to work with children and young people. You cannot apply directly to the DBS for a check and must go through a recognised 'umbrella organisation'. This might be a local volunteer bureau or the district or county council (see **Appendix 37** for contact details).

The DBS does not currently charge a fee to carry out a check for volunteers, but the umbrella organisation may do – as they need to process the application and physically see originals of your ID documents (e.g. a birth certificate). Check out what the charge is (sometimes there isn't one). Somerset has a local 'Child-Safe' organisation which is part of a national child protection scheme. Child-Safe provide free resource packs and support to groups which register on their scheme (also free) if you are not affiliated to the national governing body for a sport (e.g. the Football Association). Child-Safe can be contacted on 01823 358098 or by email at childsafe@somerset.gov.uk or have at look at the website www.child-safe.org.uk.

A sample of a staff vetting policy can be found in **Appendix 14**.

- **Risk assessment policy**

This policy needs to state how risk assessments are done, when they're done and who's responsible. It does not include the actual assessments themselves – these are carried out and reviewed (usually yearly) and kept together in a separate file, which all staff (particularly the person in charge) has access to, particularly on club nights. See the 'Health and Safety' section for more information and guidance about completing the necessary risk assessments. The Health and Safety Executive (HSE) also have lots of information about sensible risk assessment and their website is worth a look. For your convenience, **Appendix 11** contains a sample risk assessment policy and **Appendix 24** contains the HSE's *Five Steps to Risk Assessment*, which is a simple and easy to use method.

- **Health & safety policy <u>or</u> statement**

This must state how your organisation will manage health and safety in all its activities. A sample has been included in **Appendix 9**.

Please see the section on 'Health and Safety' for a clear idea of what assessments and checks you need to do to ensure that the youth club is safe.

To adopt any of these, the sample policy should be rewritten to include your club's details, agreed by the Management Committee and signed on behalf of the Management Committee by the Chairperson. You then need to ensure that the measures it mentions are in place and to make the policy available to staff, parents and young people, if they want to see it.

- **Staff employment and management policy**

If you pay staff, you really need to have one of these. It sets out how you will recruit and manage staff, how you will handle disciplinary procedures and grievances, holiday entitlement and other staff issues. **Appendix 13** gives a sample policy. If you have only unpaid staff, it is not essential, but is good practice. Please see **Section 8 'Managing paid and unpaid staff'** for more information.

5.2 Optional policies

Whilst the above policies are mandatory, there are other policies that are good practice to have. These are:

- **Equalities policy**

This policy states how your organisation will ensure that everyone that uses its services is treated fairly. Please see **Appendix 6** for a sample.

- **Fire prevention policy and procedures**

This document states how you will manage fire risks and evacuation procedures. Please see **Appendix 22** for a sample.

- **First aid policy**

This policy states how you will manage first aid in your youth club. Whilst it is not essential that all staff (or any) are first aid trained, it makes sense to ensure that at least one staff member at each session is trained. Please see **Appendix 7** for a sample.

- **Training policy**

This policy states how you will ensure that all staff (whether paid or unpaid) will be adequately trained to do what you are asking them to. Please see **Appendix 15** for a sample.

- **Code of conduct for adults working with young people**

This gives anyone working with young people a clear idea about what is expected of them. Please see **Appendix 3** for a sample.

- **ICT policy**

If you're going to give young people access to computers or the internet, it is best to have one of these. Please see **Appendix 10** for a sample.

- **Drugs and alcohol policy**

This sets out the organisation's attitude to, and response to, the use of drugs and alcohol during their youth club or on their premises. Please see **Appendix 5** for a sample.

- **Smoking policy**

This sets out the organisation's attitude to, and response to, smoking during their youth club or on their premises. Please see **Appendix 12** for a sample.

As with mandatory policies, to adopt any of these the sample policy should be rewritten to include your club's details, and be agreed by the Management Committee and signed on behalf of the Management Committee by the Chairperson. You then need to ensure that the measures it mentions are in place and give it to staff. You also need to make the policy available to parents and young people, if they want to see it.

5.3 Paperwork

The amount of paperwork that is used in the youth club is, in the main, up to your organisation. Please ensure that any paperwork containing personal information is securely kept and not shared with inappropriate people. Again, there is some paperwork that you must have and some that it is good to have.

Please see the **'Health and Safety'** section for the paperwork to record the health and safety work that needs to be carried out. This

SOMERSET County Council

5. Policies and paperwork

5. Policies and paperwork

section deals with paperwork other than that associated with health and safety.

- **Signing-in sheet**

This will help with knowing who is in the building at any time and is also useful when trying to work out how many young people actually use the youth club. It's also useful in case of fire, so that you know who is in the building (it is mentioned in the Fire Prevention and Procedures Policy Sample). See **Appendix 59** for a sample signing-in sheet.

- **Tuck sheet**

If you are running a coffee bar, a tuck sheet is useful for recording what has been sold. It is useful for stock taking and making sure the monies taken are correct. See **Appendix 60** for a sample.

- **Accident and incident report**

This replaces the old accident book. It is used to record anything untoward that happens at the youth club, in case someone complains, a parent wants more information or (if someone is injured) an investigation happens. Incidents/accidents can range from a fight, to someone banging their head, to a visit from an unhappy member of the public. One form can do all these jobs. Keep a file containing all reports in a secure place and have a couple of blanks available (just in case) for all youth club sessions. Please see **Appendix 16** for a sample incident and accident report form.

- **Sessional recording sheet**

It is useful to record what's happened at each youth club session, so that staff can see how the club and the young people are developing. It's particularly useful if there are changes in staff (for example, if a volunteer rota is being used) so that staff can find out what happened at the last few sessions. It is also helpful in monitoring any young person/people who are behaving badly. It's also a good store of information when you are looking to publicise and celebrate the club's achievements over the past six months or year.

All staff should be involved in completing the form at the end of the session. A sample recording sheet can be found in **Appendix 58**.

- **Parental consent – youth club attendance**

It is good practice to get written consent from parents for their son's/daughter's attendance at your youth club. This way, they know what their child is doing and you have emergency contact details for the parents should anything go wrong. These should be redone annually. Completed forms should be kept securely (as they contain personal details) but always be at the club when it is open. A sample annual consent form can be found in **Appendix 18**.

30

- **Parental consent – visits and adventurous activities**

You must get parental consent if you are taking young people off site and/or doing anything adventurous with them (for example, canoeing, climbing or go-karting). You also must have parental consent if you are taking young people away overnight. It is best that this consent is written. Letters asking for parental consent need to have times, places and information about the activities that are being undertaken. It's best to include too much information rather than too little, as consent must be informed (that is, parents know what they are giving consent for). Always give out two copies of the consent form, one for the parents to keep, one for them to sign and return to the club.

Completed forms should be kept securely (as they contain personal details) but be taken on the visit by staff. A sample visit consent form can be found in **Appendix 29**. Whilst it sounds harsh, it is best to have a 'no consent form, no trip' rule for young people – they will soon get used to bringing forms back if they miss a trip through not having returned a consent form. If you take young people with only verbal parental consent, you are making yourself vulnerable to legal challenge, should anything go wrong.

- **Roles and responsibilities sheet**

If the youth club is going to have a programme of interesting activities, it is useful to have a sheet that clearly says what is going to happen each week and who is going to arrange each activity and deliver it. The roles and responsibilities sheet shows exactly who is doing what. It's best to complete these sheets when the programme is agreed with staff and give everyone a copy. A sample roles and responsibilities sheet can found in **Appendix 45**.

- **Programme poster**

It's a good idea to have a poster displaying the youth club's programme, so that young people can see what's going on and be encouraged to come. Eye-catching posters can be made on most word processing packages and a sample can be found in **Appendix 57**.

Appendix 1 gives a list of the admin that most clubs use. It is here as an *aide-mémoire*.

6. Insurance

There are various types of insurance that youth clubs can have –
some are required, some are optional.

6.1 Public liability insurance

This insurance will cover claims made for injury or death of a
participant, or damage to someone else's property as a result of youth
club activity. It will also cover the legal costs and expenses associated
with such an action. This includes accidents that happen as a result of
staff negligence. It is essential that you have this insurance.

Claims can be expensive and the limit of cover will apply to claims
arising from a single incident. It is advisable to have cover for a
minimum of £5,000,000 for any one incident.

Affiliation to Somerset Rural Youth Project (SRYP) – provides
access to insurers that understand and specialise in cover for
voluntary youth clubs. For many insurers, affiliation with a local
infrastructure group (such as SRYP) is a prerequisite for getting
insurance – see **Section 15 'Support available from Somerset
County Council and other organisations'** for contact details.

Remember to be completely honest with your insurers, read their
terms and conditions and abide by any requirement, for example to
be affiliated to a local infrastructure organisation, or having written
policies or risk assessments. The insurer may refuse to meet a claim
if you haven't been truthful or fulfilled your side of the bargain.

6.2 Employer's liability insurance

If you have employees – whether paid or voluntary – you must have
employer's liability insurance. This covers you against claims for
injury, disease or death to employees, whilst in your employment.
Volunteers count as employees and therefore, even if you are
running your club solely with volunteers, the club should have this
cover. Again, affiliation to SRYP gives access to companies that
understand youth clubs and can provide this insurance.

You are legally required to insure for a minimum of £5,000,000 cover,
but most policies insure for up to £10,000,000. You must exhibit your
certificate of employer's liability insurance in the youth club.

6.3 Buildings and contents insurance

It's a good idea to insure your building and contents in case of
damage. The more insurance cover you have (particularly for

accidental damage to equipment) the higher the annual cost, so it's worth working out what you really need. Again, Somerset Rural Youth Project can put you in touch with companies that can provide this insurance.

6.4 Personal accident

This provides compensation for accidents or incidents (not caused through negligence) that cause personal injury, death or loss of equipment. This is not something that youth clubs usually offer, but if you're taking young people away overnight, or organising adventurous activities, you should remind parents that you don't provide it and that they may want to arrange it for themselves.

6.5 Insurance providers

The following are companies that commonly provide youth club insurance:

BJK Insurance Brokers,
2nd Floor, Devonshire House,
Riverside Rd, Barnstaple
Devon EX31 1EY
01271 346711
www.bjkinsurance.co.uk

Club Cover,
Lockton Insurance,
The St Botolph Building,
138 Houndsditch,
London, EC3A 7AG
0845 602 2674
www.club-cover.co.uk

Youthsure,
Jardine Lloyd Thompson,
6 Crutched Friars,
London EC3N 2PH
0800 2802818
www.youthsure.co.uk

Northern Counties Insurance
NCi House, Lowreys Lane,
Low Fell Gateshead,
Tyne & Wear NE9 5JB
0800 046 1446
www.ncinsurance.co.uk

6. Insurance

Unity Insurance Services
Lancing Business Park
Lancing
West Sussex
BN15 8UG
0845 0945 702
www.unityinsuranceservices.co.uk

This information is provided in good faith with no recommendation implied for any organisation or provider. Other insurance providers are available.

7. Health and safety in youth work

It is important, obviously, to ensure youth work activities are safe, both for young people attending them and the staff running them. Having a good health and safety track record also reassures parents who may want to encourage their children to attend the youth club.

In terms of running youth clubs, the main piece of legislation is **The Health and Safety at Work Act**. This act sets out the general duties of employers and employees. It also places a duty on those running non-domestic premises to ensure that their premises are safe, as far as is practicable. There is also a civil law duty of care to people using the premises. Being negligent (not taking reasonable care) could lead to an injured person making a claim – one reason why you must have adequate insurance cover (see the **'Insurance'** section).

Health and safety in youth work falls into two main categories:

- Safety in the club
- Safety in off-site activities

7.1 Safety in the youth club

Please see **Section 10 'Building management'** for information about building safety. It also contains information about running your own building or hiring a venue from someone else and making sure that it's safe to run a youth club from.

- **Activity risk assessment**

Apart from the safety of the venue, the other thing to consider is the safety of the activities that you are doing with the young people who come to your club. In the same way that you need to risk assess your use of a building, you'll need to do a risk assessment of your activities. **Appendix 30** contains a 'youth club general risk assessment for activities' sample, which is a starting point. If you put on activities or one-off things at the youth club, you'll need to write a separate risk assessment for each of these. A sample single activity risk assessment can be found in **Appendix 17**.

- **Staff skills and knowledge**

It's also important that your staff (paid or unpaid) are suitably skilled to do the job you're asking them to. At the very least, they need to understand the policies of your organisation, have seen and

7. Health and safety

understood the risk assessments they are working with and are familiar with the building. This can all be done in an induction meeting prior to their starting at the club. It is also recommended that all staff have a DBS check. Please see **Section 5. 'Policies and paperwork'** for more information on this and **Section 8. 'Managing paid and unpaid staff'** for information on staff management and training.

- **Parental consent**

Whilst it is legal for young people to attend your club without parental consent, it is much better to have it. Having parental consent means that you can be sure parents are informed (and much less likely to complain) about what you are doing with their children. An annual consent form (see **Appendix 18** for a sample) can cover routine youth club activities. It will also give you contact details for parents in case of accident or emergency. It is also a good idea to have any necessary medical information from parents; there is a sample form in **Appendix 26**. Completed forms should be kept securely (as they contain personal details) but always be at the club when it is open.

If you are doing an activity in the youth club that could be considered adventurous or hazardous and isn't covered by the annual consent form, you'll need to get separate consent from parents to do it. You can base the activity consent form on the annual consent form sample in **Appendix 18**.

- **First aid**

It's good practice (but not essential) to have a trained first aider at each youth club session, but all staff must know where the first aid box is! If the building doesn't have a phone, ensure a member of staff has a mobile phone (check it gets a signal) that they are happy to use, in case of emergency.

- **A word about fire drills...**

Please remember to do regular fire drills with the young people who go to the youth club (this is in the health and safety in buildings calendar in **Appendix 25**). This will make evacuation much easier in an emergency. If you run two different nights, with different groups, each should do a termly fire drill. Make it fun and offer a prize for best behaviour – they can be enjoyable!

- **Staff to young people ratios**

There is no hard and fast rule about how many staff you need to supervise young people at youth club. It all depends on:

- Size of the building
- Layout of the building
- Activities that young people are engaged (or not) in
- Behaviour of the young people
- Skills and experience of staff

It is possible to run a village youth club, with 30 or so young people attending, with two staff. This is possible if the club is in one large room, the activities are low risk, the staff are skilled and experienced and the behaviour of the young people is assessed as good – to the extent that, if there was an emergency, they would be a help rather than a hindrance. For some clubs, however, four staff may be needed for 15 young people because the building is big and sprawling with a risky outside space and the young people are not (as yet) very trustworthy. It all depends! However, as a rule it is advisable to have a minimum of three staff at all times, and more if the building is large, the attendance high or behaviour difficult.

7.2 Safety in off-site activities, including residential trips

The principles for making sure off-site activities are safe are very similar to those on site:

- **Risk assessments**
You need to make sure that where you're taking the young people is suitable and that they are appropriately managed/supervised when they are there. If you take young people to a public organised activity (for example, cinema, bowling or Alton Towers) it is safe to assume the place and activity are safe. So, in terms of risk assessments, you'll need to do one if you're transporting the young people there and one for how you will supervise them whilst they're there. It is worth noting that young people do not always need constant supervision – if they are old enough and responsible enough they can be allowed to go off on their own, as long as they can contact you should they need to and you meet them now and then. See **Appendices 27, 21** and **19** for sample minibus, coach and a bowling/McDonald's trip risk assessments.

It is easiest to keep risk assessments specific, rather than lumping them into one document. For example, if you're going on a cinema trip, do a separate risk assessment for minibus travel and another for being at the cinema, rather than putting them together into a cinema trip risk assessment. That way, if you then go bowling, you can reuse the minibus risk assessment (providing it's still relevant) and just have to do another for bowling.

- **Parental consent**
You'll need to get separate consent from parents to take young people away (even if it's not overnight), as this is not a usual youth club activity. Please see **Appendix 29** for a sample visit consent form. Please make sure that you list what the young people will be doing, particularly if it is adventurous or hazardous, as parents must know what they are consenting to. It's not enough to just state something

7. Health and safety

like 'outdoor activities', you need be clear; for example, state 'team games, swimming and abseiling' if that's what you're doing.

Always take a list of parents' contact details away with you (in case of emergencies) and a list of any allergies or medical conditions of the young people. If you're taking young people away overnight, it's best to ask parents to complete a medical form too. See **Appendix 26** for a sample medical consent form. You'll need to include how young people will be accommodated and supervised overnight in the risk assessment for the trip. See **Appendix 28** for a sample risk assessment that can be used if you're taking a group away overnight; this one is for an activity centre (for example PGL or Kilve Court).

- **Emergency contact**

It's a good idea to have someone who isn't going on the trip (but is connected to the club and has a DBS check) to have an itinerary, a list of the young people and staff on the trip, along with medical information and parents' contact details, in case anything does go wrong. They can then phone parents, leaving the staff free to deal with the incident. They could even collect young people early, in case of a home emergency, or bad behaviour.

- **Trip staffing levels**

When considering staffing for an overnight trip, it's good to have a minimum of three staff if you can, and a mix of male and female staff, if you're taking away male and female young people. It is not safe to take a group of young people away with only one staff member.

8. Managing paid and unpaid staff

Some youth clubs run solely with paid staff, some solely with volunteers and some with a mixture of the two. What follows is aimed at both paid and unpaid staff. Where there is a difference (for example with employment law) it will be clearly stated.

It is a good idea, whether staff are paid or unpaid, to have a staff employment and management policy. This sets out clearly how staff can expect to be treated. A sample is given in **Appendix 13**.

If you have a mixture of paid and unpaid staff, it is generally best to treat both types in the same way, otherwise your volunteers may feel put upon or your paid staff undervalued.

Business Link (www.gov.uk/browse/employing-people) has lots of detailed information on different aspects of employing staff and is worth looking at.

8.1 Recruiting staff

When looking for paid or unpaid youth workers, advertising in local papers, newsletters and shops is sensible (see **Appendix 31** for a sample advert). Contact with volunteer bureaus, and asking parents can often help recruit volunteer staff.

- It's useful to have a brief information sheet to go with the application form and job description. For a sample application pack information sheet, see **Appendix 34**.
- If you are paying staff you will need a job description and person specification (see **Appendices 41, 42** and **43** for samples), however it is helpful to have a job description for unpaid staff too – this way there is clarity about what you expect them to do.
- The **Appendices** contain job descriptions and person specifications for a worker to be in charge and manage the youth club, one for a level 3 qualified part-time youth worker and one for a youth support worker (an entry-level youth work post that requires little experience).
- Applicants will need to fill in an application form – this will enable you to choose who to interview and get an idea of previous skills and experience. Please see **Appendix 32** for a sample form. It is a good idea to get prospective volunteers to complete this too as it gives important information about them.

8. Managing staff

Always interview prospective unpaid staff – it will give you a good idea about whether they are suitable to work at your youth club, and give them the chance to ask questions about the club and how it works. If you are interviewing for a paid post, you should hold a fair interview process, noting the reasons for your decision. In any interview:

- You should **not** ask personal questions, for example, about family circumstance or sexual orientation.
- In interviews where you are seeing more than one applicant, you should ensure you ask all candidates the same questions.
- It's a good idea to involve at least one young person in the interview panel as they can give a view about how well the person will relate to other young people.

A set of sample interview questions can be found in **Appendices 38, 39** and **40**. One sample is for a member of staff to be in charge and manage the youth club, one is for a level 3 qualified youth worker and one is for a youth support worker. The questions are written for a youth club that is providing youth work, not positive activities.

To tailor the questions to a positive activity youth club, take out the ones that relate to learning opportunities, having a say in the running of the youth club and young people's issues.

Interviews for volunteer staff can be more informal, but still need to help you and them decide whether the role is right for them. So while it may feel more like a conversation than an interview you should make sure they get information about the club, what it does and what would be expected of them.

For paid staff particularly, there needs to be a proper record of the recruitment process, so it's important to keep the interview question sheets with application forms and references. These records must be kept securely.

Paid staff require a statement of employment to ensure the club meets its duties under employment law and to make it clear what is expected. See **Appendix 35** for a sample. **Appendix 36** is a shorter sample that can be used if the club adopts the sample staff management and employment policy in **Appendix 13**.

It is useful for volunteers to have some form of written agreement to help make sure they understand what's expected of them and that they take the role seriously. See **Appendix 44** for a sample volunteer memorandum of understanding that can be used.

8.2 Training

If you're employing staff, you can specify whether or not you want them to have a qualification in youth work (usually recognised by the Joint Negotiating Committee, which oversees professional training in youth work). Most volunteers will not have a qualification. A variety of organisations provide part-time youth work training, some of which is subsidised where funding allows. Please ring Somerset Centre for Integrated Learning (SCIL) on 01823 368280 for more information. It is not essential to have qualified youth workers to run your youth club, but it does help to ensure a certain quality of delivery.

Most staff will require further training in areas such as child protection, first aid and food hygiene as this training has a 'shelf-life' – please see **Section 5 'Policies and paperwork'** to see if your staff would need this training. It is good practice to have at least one member of staff trained in each of these areas, but it does depend on what your policies say. Again, contact SCIL to find out what training is available.

8.3 Staff meetings

Staff meetings are good places to discuss what's happening at the youth club, plan for the future and communicate important information. Even if all staff work together all the time, there usually isn't enough time during evening sessions for staff to communicate well.

It is good to have a two hour staff meeting on an evening the club isn't open, at least once a term (it's better to have one twice a term, but staff may not have the time). Notes should be taken (particularly if staff are being allocated things to do). Paid staff need to be paid for attendance. Staff meetings are usually run by the person in charge of the youth work sessions, but it is good to have someone from the management committee there too, to ensure the committee know what's happening. It is also good practice for the staff member in charge of youth work sessions to attend management committee/appropriate council meetings to provide a report on the youth club.

A sample agenda for a staff meeting might be:

1. Apologies
2. Notes of last meeting and action points
3. Evaluation of the last programme: What have the young people learnt? What did they enjoy? What would we do again?
4. Planning the next 6/12 weeks (including deciding who will do what)
5. Problems/issues/celebrations about the young people who attend

6. News from the management committee/about the town or village/upcoming opportunities
7. Any other business

Meetings are generally informal and it would be good to invite any young people who are senior members or helpers along. However, remember not to discuss issues about specific young people or families in front of them (as this could cause confidentiality problems).

8.4 Supervision

The staff member in charge of running the youth club should be supervised by whichever adult group is responsible for it. This is usually the management committee, but could be a parish or town council. It is common practice that the lead 'youth' officer from the management committee (or council) meets the staff member in charge of the youth club once every two months to discuss the club in a structured way. Set aside two hours for this, and make sure notes are taken. This is essential whether staff are paid or not, to help ensure the adult group is aware of what is happening in the club they are ultimately responsible for, and the worker feels supported. A sample supervision record sheet is included in **Appendix 46.** If staff are being paid, you must supervise staff, or ensure they are being supervised.

A sample agenda for a supervision meeting might be:

1. Actions agreed from last supervision – update
2. Update from the youth club (including how the programme is going, number of young people attending, the behaviour of young people, how young people are being involved in making decisions at the club)
3. Finances – what has been spent, what money is needed
4. Staffing – brief update on paid staff and volunteers, how they are doing and any issues
5. Projects planned/upcoming events
6. Training needs
7. Any other business

The supervisor and staff member usually contribute to supervision agendas.

Whilst supervision is very important, the supervisor also needs to be available for contact by the staff member in charge. This may be weekly, usually by telephone and is a way of keeping up to date.

It is equally important that the staff (paid or unpaid) who work at the youth club are, in turn, supervised by the staff member in charge. Again, this should be once every two months, but only for an hour.

A sample agenda may be:

1. Actions agreed from last supervision – update
2. How do you think youth club is going?
3. Update/discussions about any projects they are responsible for
4. Training needs
5. Action planning
6. Any other business

Again, both the staff member in charge of the club and staff member should contribute to the supervision agenda.

If there are a large number of volunteers, it may be better to have small group (about three or four staff) supervisions to save time.

8.5 Poor staff performance

If a member of staff is performing poorly, the first thing to do is raise it in supervision and agree how the member of staff should be performing. This is then monitored. In the majority of cases, a friendly word in supervision is enough for staff to improve. Unfortunately, you may get to the point where you feel that you need to formally discipline staff. The process for doing this should be listed in either a staff employment and management policy (see **Appendix 13**) or in their statement of employment (see **Appendix 35**). It would be wise to seek further advice at this stage, unless you (or one of the management committee) already have human resource management experience.

8.6 Keeping staff records

If you employ staff (whether paying them yourself or through a payroll service) there are some records you must keep and some it is good practice to keep.

You **must** keep staff-related records on:

- Pay rates – to meet the statutory requirement to issue workers with pay statements and to ensure you are paying your workers at least the national minimum wage
- Payroll – i.e. on income tax and National Insurance deductions for HM Revenue & Customs
- Sickness of more than four days and how much statutory sick pay you have paid

SOMERSET County Council

8. Managing staff

- Accidents, injuries and dangerous occurrences – to meet health and safety requirements (you can do this using the accident and incident form sample in **Appendix 16**)

You must also keep records to ensure that weekly working time and night work limits (under the Working Time Regulations) are complied with. Asking staff to complete time recording sheets (see **Appendix 49**) will cover this, as well as enabling you to keep a check on what hours staff are working.

It's also good practice to keep records of each worker's:

- Training
- Employment history – date employment began, promotions, job title(s)
- Absence – records of lateness, sickness, and any other authorised or unauthorised absences
- Personal details – name, address, emergency phone number(s), qualifications, work-relevant disability
- Terms and conditions of employment – including a copy of each employee's written statement and correspondence relating to any changes to their terms and conditions

More generally, you should keep written records (e.g. minutes) of:

- Supervision meetings
- Any disciplinary action you have ever taken, in particular disciplinary hearings
- Individual and collective redundancy consultation meetings and agreements

Keeping staff records beyond those required by law may help you to: avoid or defend employment tribunal claims if a dispute with a worker arises; assess the performance of individual workers; ensure you are treating job applicants and workers consistently and fairly; make decisions in relation to staffing levels, e.g. on recruitment and redundancy.

Under data protection legislation, any personal information you keep on your staff should be adequate, relevant and not excessive. Inadequate records can lead to problems when dealing with absence levels, staff turnover, sickness, lateness and discipline.

8.7 Extra requirements for paid staff

If you use paid staff there are greater requirements than is the case for a purely volunteer-led club.

A policy will be required to outline how staff are recruited, paid, managed and trained. This could be called the 'staff employment and management policy' or something similar. It will also need to cover how you will manage any disciplinary situation and the grounds on which a staff member can be dismissed. Please see **Appendix 13** for a sample policy.

For PAYE and tax information, please look at **Section 4 'Money matters'**.

8.8 Payroll services

Where a club doesn't have its own payroll system this can be dealt with through a payroll bureau. The services available vary and it is worth spending time to make sure you find a supplier that can meet your needs. Information about suppliers of payroll services that can help small youth groups is provided in **Appendix 47**.

8.9 Using self-employed contractors or companies

Where paid staff are self-employed (sole trader) or have a registered company, then they are responsible for their own tax affairs. In this way you can save having to run a payroll system and just pay each month (or quarter) on receipt of invoices (in the same way you would for a decorator painting the club). Please see the **PAYE and tax section in Section 4 'Money matters'** for more information.

You will still need to keep staff records. In this situation you need to be clear about what is expected of the worker, their hours, who they report to, etc.

If you decide to employ a company, please refer to **Section 9 'Out-sourcing your youth work'** for more information.

9. Outsourcing your youth work

9.1 The pros and cons

If you decide not to directly employ your own staff, you can choose to employ a company or charity to deliver youth work in your club. There are pros and cons to this solution. The pros are:

- You don't have to manage or supervise staff
- You don't have to find cover for staff sickness and holidays
- You're not responsible for making sure that the staff have the proper skills and training
- You can stipulate what you want and ask the company to provide reports on whether or not they are achieving it
- You don't have to provide payroll, you just pay an invoice
- If you choose the right company, you'll get a very professional service with very little hassle

The cons are:

- It will usually be more expensive, as you will be paying the company to do management things that you would be doing yourself (usually voluntarily) if you were employing staff
- You don't have so much control over what actually happens during the sessions, as you're not directly managing them
- You'll need to create a service specification saying what you want, rather than 'feeling your way' through it (if you were managing it yourself), and create a contract
- If you want to ensure value for money, you'll have to go through a selection process

Youth work providers can be private companies, social enterprises, or charities.

9.2 The selection process

If you choose to employ a company or charity, a good process to follow is:

- Write a service specification (see **Appendix 48** for a sample).
- Advertise the opportunity (a good place is via the CHYPPS/Vista website www.commissioningtogether.org.uk) and ask for expressions of interest.

- Send out the specification to those who contact you to express their interest and give a two week deadline for the company or charity to return their application. Also give an interview date.
- Shortlist from the applications and invite the chosen candidate providers for interview.
- Interview the candidate providers – you can ask different questions to each (unlike when you're interviewing for a job) and questions should be based on their application forms and your service specification.
- Choose the provider you want to deliver the contract, notify them in writing and get the contracts signed (see **Appendix 33** for a sample). After a two week reflection period (for both parties to change their minds in they wish), you're good to go.

9.3 What to look for in a provider

When making a decision about which provider to use, the following gives a guide of what to look for:

- A financially robust company which won't go under in the middle of the contract
- Previous experience of delivering what your club wants
- Qualified and experienced staff
- Appropriate insurances and policies
- What the company can offer in terms of 'value added' – over and above what you ask for in your specification
- Price (if you don't state this up front)
- Hidden costs (such as programme costs, travel costs)
- Size of the management fee/'profit'

If you like what a potential provider offers, but they're charging a bit more than you wanted to pay, always find out whether they are willing to come down in price. It's a bit like haggling – you never know until you ask.

9.4 Finding a provider

Alternatively, if you know of a good local provider (recommendations are good) you may wish to only offer the work to them. In this case, using a clear service specification is still strongly recommended, as it provides clarity for everyone. Somerset Youth and Community Service holds a list of youth work providers with brief information about their policies and procedures. Please contact SYCS on 01823 349852 for more information.

9.5 Bigger contracts

If your contract is worth over £25,000 it may be that you want to go through a more complex process to ensure the best possible provider. Again, please contact SCYS on 01823 349852 for more information.

10. Building management

Most management committees already manage buildings and are good at it. It is a complex area and advice should be sought if you are unsure of anything. Somerset Youth and Community Service can offer advice and guidance on building management issues (telephone 01823 349852). This chapter gives guidance on building management, including health and safety requirements, hiring out premises to other groups to raise funds and using someone else's premises to deliver youth work. Please see **Section 6 'Insurance'** for information about the types of insurance that are needed and a list of suppliers.

10.1 Ensuring your building is fit for use

It is the management committee's responsibility to ensure that the building is safe to use for the youth club and all other users. This includes checking fixtures and fittings, having risk assessments for the building and arson prevention and being available to sort out problems.

Attached in **Appendix 25** is a health and safety in buildings calendar, listing the health and safety items that should be checked, the regularity of the checks and a format to record the checks have been carried out. It is very important that the checks are recorded because, in the event of an incident, these are the proof that the management committee have met their responsibility to provide a safe building. As well as these checks, it is important that the building is visited once a week to ensure that nothing has been broken or is causing a potential hazard – this can be done by the youth workers! It also helps ensure that routine maintenance is carried out to prevent general building issues getting to crisis point.

It is also important that the management committee responds to reports of breakages or repairs needed, as again this counts towards providing a safe environment. A communication book that lives behind the coffee bar or in the office, which all users have access to, is useful for minor problems. A contact number for the management committee needs to be on display in the office or coffee bar for the more serious, or immediate problems. A communication book is just a bound book of blank pages with 'Communication Book' written on the front, that user groups are aware of. It can also be used for the different groups to communicate with each other, should they be getting in each others' way.

10.2 Building risk assessments

The management committee should provide a risk assessment (including arson prevention) for the use of the building – a sample is attached in **Appendix 20** – it will need to be reviewed for each building. These assessments, once made specific to the building and signed off by the management committee, should be given to user groups as they will need to abide by them too. Management committees cannot be expected to provide risk assessments for user groups' activities – this is the responsibility of the user group itself. A youth club general risk assessment sample can be found in **Appendix 30** and more is said about youth club specific health and safety in **Section 7** '**Health and safety in youth work**'.

10.3 Signage

The management committee must maintain appropriate signage in their building. This includes fire exits, the location of fire extinguishers and the first aid kit, fire evacuation procedures and bomb alerts. **Appendix 23** gives a sample first aid and fire procedure sign. Signage that complies with legislation for fire exits etc can be found cheaply on the internet. Search for 'health and safety signs'.

10.4 Building licences and registrations

There are some activities that, if you are doing them (or allowing them to be done) in your building, you must have a licence for, or register for. These include:

- Playing recorded music or allowing live music to be played: there are two organisations that provide licences for this, The Performing Rights Society (PRS – www.prsformusic.com) and Phonographic Performance Limited (PPL – www.ppluk.com). PPL collects and distributes licence fees for the use of recorded music on behalf of record companies and performers, while PRS collects and distributes for the use of musical compositions and lyrics on behalf of songwriters, composers and publishers. It is likely you will need licences from both organisations. Visit their websites for more details.
- Showing films from DVD or other recorded source: the Motion Picture Licensing Corporation (www.themplc.co.uk) collects and distributes licence fees on behalf of film producers and publishers. You will need a licence to show DVDs from all the major film and TV production companies.
- If you have a kitchen (even if you only make tea and coffee) you must register with the environmental health department at your district council. See **Appendix 61** for their contact details.

10. Building management

10. Building management

- Public buildings need to be licensed for 'regulated entertainment' (for example, live bands, parties, bingo, dance, discos, sports etc.). Again, you should contact your district council for more information.
- Don't forget your TV licence. This is a requirement even if you watch programmes from the internet. Visit www.tvlicencing.co.uk for more information.

If you are renting space in someone else's building, make sure the owners of the building have the correct licences and registrations.

10.5 Hiring out your building

It is important that if the building the committee is responsible for is being hired out to other users, a proper agreement is in place. The agreement needs to be clear about the price, what is included in the hiring arrangement and who is responsible for what. **Appendix 51** provides a conditions of hire agreement and **Appendix 50** contains a sample booking form.

Don't forget to publicise the Communications Book and give each new user a personal induction to the building. Inside the Communications Book, it's a good idea to have a list of useful numbers and the location of useful items (such as stopcocks etc). A sample list can be found in **Appendix 52**.

It's also a good idea, if you have three or more regular groups hiring out your building, to hold user group meetings (they may also be interested in joining the management committee). That way, you can keep them up to date with any developments, issues or problems and they can do the same with you. It's also good to sort out any niggles the different users may have with each other. Keep minutes and send them out.

10.6 Renting space to house your youth club

If you need to hire premises to deliver your youth work (village halls are popular for this), make sure you have a hirer's agreement as this will set out what your responsibilities and expectations are. If you are unsure of any conditions, ask for a response in writing. You will still need public liability and employer's insurance. Its wise to meet the managers of the building and be very honest about what you intend to use it for – you may think you're providing a service for the community, unfortunately, some people may think you're purposely attracting undesirable elements to their area – so it's best to be clear from the start.

Ask to see the risk assessment for the building; if there isn't one or you think it isn't appropriate, you'll need to write one yourself. The building risk assessment in **Appendix 20** is a good starting point.

If there isn't a Communications Book, suggest one and make sure your staff/volunteers keep an eye on it in case someone leaves a message for the youth club. Ask your staff/volunteers to always check the building when they arrive and note any damage before they open the session. Youth clubs have a habit of being blamed for any damage, so its best in multi-use buildings to assess the state of things before the session starts. One of the reasons youth clubs get blamed for damage is that young people do occasionally (and usually accidentally) damage the building. If this happens, report it immediately, be honest and be prepared to pay for the repair. Some building managers accept a certain amount of wear and tear and others don't. Being honest cuts down on suspicion and your word will more likely be accepted if it wasn't the youth club that did something.

Always try to attend any user group meetings as it's important you're aware of any building changes or issues and that the youth club (through you) has a say in any developments. You might even convince the group to let you take a young person with you (see **Section 13** '**Involving young people in decision making and volunteering'**).

Finally, please remember that just because it isn't your building, doesn't mean you have no responsibility for health and safety. You, or your staff, must do a visual check of the building before the start of each session to ensure that it is safe to operate in – this includes checking fire escapes are clear and open, a visual check of extinguishers, and making sure that nothing is broken or badly arranged that might be a hazard for young people. It is your (or your staff's) decision about the suitability of the state of the building for each session. Any problems need to be reported to building managers and if you think the building isn't safe (for example, all the fire exits are blocked and you can't clear them) you'll need to not run the session. In this case, wait outside the building and tell young people the club is shut, as they arrive. After about half an hour, staff should leave a note on the door and can go home.

You may (and it is recommended) ask the building managers to see safety records for gas appliances, fire alarms etc., every so often (at least once a year) to satisfy yourself that the building is being managed and maintained properly.

10. Building management

11. Running your youth club

This section looks at what you need to achieve and sort out before opening your doors to young people.

11.1 What are you trying to achieve?

You're probably trying to achieve one of two things:

1. Providing a safe place for young people to go and socialise and (possibly) do interesting things (this is called a *positive activity*).

or

2. Providing a safe place for young people to go and socialise and do interesting things whilst also providing learning and development opportunities and staff that young people can talk to and get information and advice from (commonly called *youth work*).

It is more straightforward to provide a positive activity, although many of the policies and procedures are the same as when you are providing youth work. Either provision is good for young people. Many clubs start off providing positive activities and develop into providing youth work, when they've got the hang of policies and procedures.

The main difference between the two is that a positive activity is about providing somewhere for young people to go that is structured and safe. Youth work, however, aims to provide this, plus developmental learning opportunities aimed at enabling young people to reach their potential by increasing their knowledge and skills (generally through training) and giving them the opportunity to practise their skills through projects and experience. Youth work is based on the relationships staff have with young people and the trust that is built through these relationships. It also includes the provision of unbiased information and advice.

You need to decide which you are aiming for when you are setting up your youth club as it will affect the programme you offer and the skills you need staff (paid or unpaid) to have.

11.2 Chain of command (or who's in charge?)

Before doing anything else, it's important to be clear about who is in charge of what. This comes in two parts – who is in charge of each youth club session that is delivered and who is responsible, on the management committee, for managing staff, adopting policies, arranging for insurances, paying bills and fundraising. Please see **Section 3 'The management committee'** for information about who is responsible for what on the management committee.

In terms of the youth club sessions, you should have a named person who is officially in charge of the session. All staff (and young people) need to know who this is. The staff member in charge is the person to make all the decisions in an emergency (such as a fire evacuation or injury) and to co-ordinate the work of the other staff. The staff member in charge has the final say in any disputes or issues that arise during the session. It is best if this is always the same person. It is usually this person who will supervise and manage the other staff (see **Section 8 'Managing paid and unpaid staff'**).

If your usual staff member in charge is away, you must nominate a new one and make sure that they let the other staff and young people know. You must also make sure that the 'stand-in' is aware of their new responsibilities, particularly around health and safety.

If you are employing staff, the staff member in charge is usually paid more (in acknowledgement of their extra responsibilities) and is usually paid extra hours to do any preparation for sessions, to manage any other staff and ensure health and safety requirements are adhered to. A rule of thumb is that a staff member in charge of one session a week needs an extra hour and a half per week (on top of the set-up, opening times and clearing away time) to do these things. So, if you are opening a youth club for two and a half hours a week and delivering youth work, a staff member in charge will need to be paid for five hours. This is made up as follows:

Setting up before club opens.	¼ hour
Delivery time whilst the club is open.	2 ½ hours
Clear up after the club shuts.	¼ hour
Plan and prepare the programme. Staff supervisions and team meetings. Health and safety in terms of building checks, risk assessments and consent forms. Organise the tuck shop.	2 hours
Total	**5 hours**

They won't always use five hours a week, some weeks will be more than others, but it will even out over the course of a year. Ask them to keep a tally of their hours each week so that you can see what they are spending their time on.

If you are delivering positive activities, the staff member in charge probably only needs to be paid for four hours a week, as there is less programme planning and research.

11. Running your youth club

11.3 Attracting young people to your youth club

Whether delivering a positive activity or youth work, you need to make sure that young people know your youth club is happening so that they can come. The best places to advertise are local shops (posters and flyers), village notice boards and through the local secondary school if possible. Many schools are happy to put up posters, but make sure you get permission first – some will even allow you to do a presentation during assemblies, but you need to book in advance. When you're up and running, you can ask young people to design your publicity (and do assemblies for you), but if you're just starting you may need to do it yourself. Design something simple and colourful giving the day, time, age range and an idea of what's on offer. A sample (created using Microsoft Word) is given in **Appendix 53**.

It is worth contacting the local paper too. Whilst young people don't generally read it, their parents do and they need to be reassured that your group is above board.

11.4 Publicity and public relations

It's important that not only young people know about the youth club – adults in your community need to know about it too. An awareness of what the club does means that you're less likely to get complaints from concerned adults and more offers of help – you may even get donations. A good public image also helps to balance up the often negative portrayal that young people get in the press.

Having a good relationship with your community can be achieved in a number of ways and needn't be hugely time consuming. Some suggestions are listed below:

- **Produce a club information sheet** that lists the name, address and telephone number of the club and a contact number (if different) for the chairperson of the management committee or youth worker in charge of sessions – this means members of the community can contact you easily if they need to. Also include the opening times and what the club aims to achieve – so that parents can see what their children are asking to go to. A sample of the programme and a list of previous club successes give a good sense of the club too. This can be included in a parish magazine and/or put up in local shops and on notice boards.

- **Send out a monthly newsletter** to let the community know what the club is doing and include some contact details for anyone interested in joining in. This is often a good project for members' groups.

- **Have a column in the town/parish newsletter**. It doesn't have to be a long one, just giving information about planned club activities, developments and contact details. Again, this could be something done by the members' group.

- **Put up a sign** outside your club that looks professional and can be easily seen by anyone looking for it. Try to match the sign to your logo, if you have one. If you don't have one, work with some young people to create one!

- **Have a stall at local events** such as community fairs or fun days. Have photos and a little text to illustrate what the club does – make sure you include any press articles about the club, as well as some flyers to give away. This could be staffed by young people.

- **Hold an open evening** where young people welcome adults in the community to come and have a look around.

- **Produce an annual report** about the club activities, successes and achievements.

- **Hold a celebration evening** where you (or your president or a local dignitary or famous person) give out prizes and certificates to the young people who have attended the youth club over the past year. Refreshments, nibbles and a presentation (let the young people use their imagination!) about what the club has been up to make a good evening.

- **The local press** is a good way of publicising your club. Press releases are a good way of communicating with them. Find out who your local reporter is and get to know them, so that you have a contact to send your press releases to. Remember to be concise and clear about your story and if you include a photo of named young people, make sure you get their parents' permission first. Make sure you invite your press contact to celebration evenings and the AGM. Finding a good local contact also applies to radio and television, but these opportunities are usually more limited.

- **Have a social media presence (Facebook page etc.)**
  The majority of young people use social media applications such as Twitter and Facebook as one of their key means of communication. It's a good idea to have a youth club presence on one or both of these applications. You'll need an understanding of how they work and it's not the remit of this handbook to explain this (and there are generally good instructions on each of these applications). Remember that you'll need to monitor what is posted on your pages and check that it's appropriate for your club, and

bear in mind that the minimum age to sign up on Facebook is 13, so don't aim your content at anyone younger. The best thing to do is to find a local volunteer who can set up and maintain this for you – young people are generally good at this! Remember that you'll need to monitor what is posted on your pages and check that it's appropriate for your club.

11.5 Setting the scene

Whether delivering a positive activity or youth work, you need to make sure that the venue that you're using is suitable.

- It needs to be warm, well lit and welcoming. It's good to have interesting posters displaying lots of diverse images of different young people if you can – it will make them all feel welcome. It helps if the décor is appealing to young people too – if you're not sure, ask some of them what they think!

- If you're using a building that is shared with other groups, you probably won't be able to redecorate, but you can put up posters, make sure it's clean and tidy away anything else other user groups have left out. It can be off-putting for young people if they are surrounded by (for example) play group equipment – also, they are likely to play with it and could break it!

- If you have games and equipment for the young people to use unsupervised (for example board games), then put these out at the start of the session.

- Always check fire exits are clear and unlocked, corridors are unobstructed and any rooms that the young people are not supposed to use are locked.

- You'll need to know that the building is safe for use too – please see **Section 7 'Health and safety in youth work'** and **Section 10 'Building management'** for a list of things you need to check when using a building.

- Finally, check for any damage before and after each session – that way, you'll only be responsible for any damage you do, crucial if you're operating in a shared building.

- It is also a good idea to make sure that copies of ground rules (see '**Managing behaviour and supervision of young people**' below) and the current programme (see '**Programme planning**' below) are clearly displayed.

- Make sure that young people have to sign in when they enter (you need to know who is in the building in case of fire and it's good to know who's coming) so assign a staff member to supervise the signing-in sheet (see **Appendix 59**) and collect any entry money (usually known as 'subs').

It's a good idea for staff to turn up at least 15 minutes before the start of a session, so they can set up the building, remind themselves about who is doing what and also read any extra risk assessments associated with the session (see **Section 7 'Health and safety in youth work'** for information about risk assessments).

11.6 Programme planning

If you're running a drop-in, you don't necessarily have to have a programme, just somewhere safe and warm with social space.

Whether delivering a positive activity or youth work, you need to have some sort of programme for your youth club. The programme content is really the main difference between youth work and positive activities. Whatever sort of programme you are planning to deliver, you need to consider the following:

- What do the young people say they want to do?
- What do staff think the young people need or want to do?
- What do you want young people to learn or achieve?
- What are staff able to deliver?
- How much will it cost, both in staff time and resources (such as money)?
- Is it inclusive? Can everyone have a go or are you thinking of specific groups (such as particular ages or genders)? If you are, can you make sure that those not included have other opportunities?
- Are there any special holidays/events that you need to include or plan around (for example Christmas, Valentine's Day, Yom Kippur, school holidays)?
- Are there things you want to encourage young people's interest in (for example community events, first aid or anti-bullying)?

A positive activity programme will be relatively simple, containing interesting activities for young people to do, if they want. It will be based on what you think the young people want to do. It includes a number of things they can do themselves and some extra, supervised activities for variety. A sample eight week programme might include:

Week	Programme
1	Pool, table tennis and Wii. Making Valentine's cards.
2	Pool, table tennis and Wii. Team Games.
3	Table tennis and Wii. Pool competition. Nail art.
4	Pool, table tennis and Wii. T-shirt decorating.
5	Pool, table tennis and Wii. Film night with popcorn.
6	Pool, table tennis and Wii. Snakes and Ladders Challenge.
7	Pool and table tennis. Karaoke night. Make a members' photo board.
8	Pool, table tennis and Wii. Make a memory box.

A youth work programme contains the same fun activities, but will also include a project or educational activity – it is based on the needs (as well as the wants) of young people. A sample eight week programme could include:

Week	Programme
1	Pool, table tennis and Wii. Making Valentine's cards. What makes a good relationship? 'Ideal partner' quiz.
2	Pool, table tennis and Wii. Team Games. Promoting the Condom Card and safer sex.
3	Table tennis and Wii. Pool competition. What do you want on the playing fields? Parish Council consultation.
4	Pool, table tennis and Wii. T-shirt decorating. Debate night – what are your views? Are you always right?
5	Pool, table tennis and Wii. International Women's Day – who inspires you?
6	Pool, table tennis and Wii. Snakes and Ladders Challenge. Smoking quiz and 'So You think You Know Cannabis' game.
7	Pool and table tennis. Karaoke night. Make a members' photo board.
8	Pool, table tennis and Wii. 'I wish I could…' exercise. Programme planning for the next eight weeks.

As you can see, it will take staff time to sort out resources to deliver a positive activities programme, and even more staff time to deliver a youth work programme. This needs to be taken into account if you're paying staff (as you need to pay preparation time) or even if you have volunteers, as someone has to volunteer to do this. It is safe to say young people get more out of youth work, but you do need to put more in.

It is good practice to expect parents to complete an annual consent form for their young people to attend your club. That way, parents know what you're doing and you know they are happy for their son/daughter to attend. This way you also have contact details for parents, should there be an accident or behaviour problem. At the very least, you must ask young people to give you parental contact information for the same reasons. Please see **Appendix 18** for a sample annual consent form.

Please remember that you can hire lots of equipment, rather than buy it. Somerset County Council provides a Youth Equipment Store where equipment can be hired for much less than commercial rates. Go to the website www.somersetyouth.co.uk and follow the Youth Equipment Store link for information about what is available, or phone 01823 410131. There is a huge variety from karaoke machines and hiking boots to Wiis and sports equipment.

11.7 Trips and activities

Young people really like to go on trips and they don't need to be complex or expensive. Young people always say they want to go to Alton Towers (which can be time consuming and cost a lot) but they also enjoy trips bowling, to the cinema, shopping or visiting other youth clubs. Always ask young people what they want to do; as if you put on a trip they're not interested in, they won't go!

Leave a good amount of time when planning a trip, this way you can ensure it's what young people want, book appropriate transport, get parental consent (you **must** do this), do the necessary risk assessments and find any extra money required to subsidise it. Please see **Section 7 'Health and safety in youth work'** for information about risk assessments. For trips you need to risk assess the journey and the supervision of young people. If you are going to a public, organised activity (for example the swimming pool or Alton Towers) you don't need to risk assess the activity as the provider will have done this. However, if you are providing the activity yourself (for example beach games or shopping) you will need to risk assess the activity. For off-site activities, you must have specific parental consent (these trips are not covered under the annual consent form). Please see **Appendix 29** for a sample trip consent form.

SOMERSET County Council

Always remember to agree ground rules prior to the trip and evaluate the trip afterwards, so you can do it better next time.

Somerset County Council currently has minibuses that can be hired at reduced rates by community groups (this is much cheaper than commercial rates). Please look on the website www.somersetyouth.co.uk for more information about bus hire or ring 01823 349852.

You will also need parental consent if you are going to do something hazardous with your group on the youth club premises – for example, hiring a climbing wall or bringing in quad bikes for use on the playing field, unless you have already listed it on your annual consent form.

11.8 Managing behaviour and supervision of young people

This is usually the subject that concerns people most. It must be said that the vast majority of young people are well-behaved for the vast majority of the time and cause no problems. However, you need to create a culture of positive behaviour in your youth club to ensure this is the case.

The first thing to do is to set basic ground rules for behaviour (this lets young people know what you expect of them) and clear sanctions for misbehaviour (this lets young people know what will happen if they break the ground rules). It's best to set positive ground rules (such as 'we will treat each other with respect') rather than negative ground rules (such as 'no fighting, shouting or swearing') as negative rules give a negative message. Proscribing what *can't* be done also means that, if you forget to proscribe something, young people can say you didn't tell them not to do something. This means you could end up with a list as long as your arm! Positive rules give a positive impression and are easier to manage.

It is best to get the young people that attend to set the ground rules and sanctions (they are usually stricter than adults) with your help. That way, they will have ownership of them and are more likely to abide by them. Always ensure you enforce the ground rules because if you ignore them, so will young people.

For hints and tips on managing behaviour, a sample ground rules and sanctions list and a sample banning and re-admittance procedure has been given in **Appendix 55**.

Please remember, most young people behave appropriately! Apart from clear and agreed ground rules, the most useful thing to manage behaviour is an interesting choice of things to do, to keep young people busy. Also, don't forget to celebrate positive behaviour, as well as having consequences for bad.

When running your youth club, you need to decide on your supervision ratios. That is to say, how many staff you need to oversee how many young people safely. This will depend on a number of things, including:

- The level of experience and expertise of your staff
- The behaviour of the young people
- The layout and size of your building
- The activities on your programme

As a rule of thumb, one member of staff to ten young people is *usually* enough (please note, this isn't a recommendation to work on your own with ten young people, this is a rule of thumb for larger groups. A recommended minimum level, even with small numbers, is two staff). **However**, the staff ratio can rise or fall depending on circumstances. For example, if you have four different rooms and an outside area, one staff member to ten young people may not be enough. If the young people are behaving very badly, this may not be enough. If you have 40 well-behaved young people in one big space and you're not doing anything hazardous, you may be safe with only two staff. This number can only be decided by you and your staff team. Remember, if things get out of hand, calling the police and/or shutting the club is always an option (although one that is very rarely needed). As a minimum, always ensure there are at least two adults even with small groups of young people – this means that you are prepared for any emergencies (such as sickness etc.).

11.9 What to do when things go wrong...

Whilst most youth club sessions are trouble free, things do occasionally go wrong and it is best to be prepared. Below are listed a few possible difficulties and some suggestions for coping with them.

- **A young person tells you they are being abused**
This is rare, but can happen as young people trust their youth workers. The Children Act 1989 places a responsibility on anyone working with children and young people to report any disclosure, or any suspicion they may have, that a young person is at risk of serious harm. Young people need to know that staff can't keep this sort of thing to themselves. A good way to prepare for this is to have a confidentiality statement displayed in the club that says that staff may not be able to keep secrets that might be harmful to young people (see **Appendix 54** for a sample). Make sure staff discuss this with all young people. If a disclosure is made (or if any staff have

suspicions that a young person is at risk of serious harm), remind the young person that you can't keep it secret, offer them support (but don't ask probing questions) and then ring Somerset Direct (0845 345 9122) for advice.

It is recommended that at least one member of staff on each session has had some child protection training (although it's better to all have done it). Contact Child-Safe for information (phone 01823 358098, email childsafe@somerset.gov.uk or via the website www.child-safe.org.uk). Alternatively, look on the Somerset Local Safeguarding Children Board website www.somersetlscb.org.uk.

- **Bad behaviour**

If behaviour gets really out of hand, ring the police and close the club. If you can, ring round parents and let them know what you've done. It's not what anyone wants to do, but you must consider the safety of all the young people in your care. It's a good idea to contact the local Police Community Support Officer (PCSO) and neighbourhood sergeant before you open and ask them to drop in for coffee now and again – this sends a clear message about the youth club not being isolated from the outside world and also builds links between young people and the police that aren't based on law breaking.

When you re-open, talk to the young people as they come in, using your ground rules to reinforce messages about behaviour. You may have had to ban young people (see the banning and re-admittance process in **Appendix 55**) so make sure there are enough staff on the door to turn young people away, if necessary.

This is a rare occurrence, but it is best to be prepared!

- **Breakages and damage to the building**

Young people at youth clubs do occasionally break or damage things. Mostly it's accidental as young people tend to be clumsier than adults. Occasionally it's deliberate or a result of foolishness. You need to work out which of these it is (sometimes you can't) and decide what sanctions you put in place and whether or not you will charge the young person (and their parents) for the cost of the damage. If you know the family can't afford it, you may negotiate some volunteering that the young person does (e.g. sweeping up or washing up at the end of the evening) as a way of 'paying' for the damage. Ensure that whatever course of action you decide upon is fair and can be explained to the other young people attending. Sometimes, it's a good idea to ask young people what they think ought to be done (be careful of this as they can be a bit harsh).

There will always be wear and tear on equipment and the building, so make sure you budget for this because there are always accidents and it is harsh to expect young people to pay every time.

If you are in a shared building and the equipment damaged does not belong to you, or the young people have damaged the building itself, make sure you let the owners know as soon as possible. Nothing sours a relationship quicker than unexplained damage! Do a thorough check at the end of each session (even if it's been quiet) to check nothing is amiss.

- **Injury**

It's good practice to have a qualified first aider working on each session. If a young person is injured during your session, give them first aid and then (depending on the severity of the injury) let them carry on, call their parents or call an ambulance. Make sure you record the incident. You can use the accident and incident report form in **Appendix 16**. Always contact the parents and let them know what's happening.

11.10 Recording sessions

It is important to record what happens at each youth work session. Session recordings help to:

- Identify trends in the club
- Remind staff how successful an activity was
- Brief staff on what has happened if they have been away or if you operate a volunteer rota system
- Create good reports for the management group/funders about what has happened over the months
- Enable staff to reflect on what they did well and not so well that evening
- Inform future planning

It is best to allow 15 minutes after the youth club shuts for staff to reflect on the session and complete the recording sheet. A sample can be found in **Appendix 58**.

11. Running your youth club

12. From positive activities to youth work

Many youth clubs provide positive activities and are happy to do so. They are providing an important service to their communities. Delivering positive activities requires less preparation time from staff, less organisation from managers and a less skilled (but no less enthusiastic) workforce. This means that it's easier to manage and easier to provide.

However, what some clubs find is that, when delivering a safe warm place for young people to go and giving them something to do, the young people seem to want more. The following things *may* happen:

- Young people build trusting relationships with the staff at the youth club and want to tell them personal things, or get information and advice from them
- Staff at youth clubs, during conversations with young people, notice that some young people don't know some things, or are ignorant of important information and want to help them learn
- Young people come up with good ideas for projects and want to make these ideas reality
- Young people want to take more responsibility in the youth club
- Young people want to make changes in their communities and want staff at the youth club to help them

These are the reasons that some youth clubs develop from positive activities into youth work.

If these things do happen, you can continue to deliver positive activities. Many youth clubs do, because they do not have the capacity to do anything more than that. And, as previously stated, providing a positive activity is a very important service for young people in the community.

If, however, you decide you want to develop your positive activity youth club into providing youth work, you don't need to do it all at once. Below are listed some things that you might want to do, to develop your youth club from a positive activity provider to a youth work provider.

12.1 Information and advice for young people

If your staff want to give good information and advice to young people, the best (and easiest) place to start is the internet (see

Appendix 61 for a list of useful websites). There are many websites that give good information about all sorts of issues, from health advice to legal issues to employment skills. Many of the websites offer downloadable resources that staff can use, including quizzes, project ideas and games. It is important to check the provider of the content. Government websites are a good place to start. Many youth clubs link into national campaigns and provide information to young people, for example, the NHS provides free resources to support No Smoking Day. Do make sure that staff vet any leaflets or information available to young people to ensure that it's appropriate – it's useful to think about how you would justify giving out a particular leaflet if a parent complained.

Find out what other people are out there to help young people. There may be health professionals, or employment specialists, or other trained people around who are happy to come and see young people at your club. Make a list of those in your area.

There are often training opportunities for staff who work with young people to get information and ideas about particular issues. These can be whole courses or a single day's training. Contact Somerset Youth and Community Service on 01823 349852 for more information.

12.2 Project work with young people

If young people, or staff, come up with a good idea for a project at your youth club, and the youth club has the time and resources to support it, go ahead with the project! Some things to remember are:

- Ensure your project is achievable, with some early success to keep young people interested.
- Plan *with* the young people, do not present them with a whole project. Young people are more likely to see things through if they are part of creating the project. Listen to their ideas and use your experience to help make the plans a reality. Sometimes, you have to let young people make their own mistakes as they don't believe your experiences!
- Set a budget and have regular budget updates with the young people.
- Remember that young people have busy lives and the youth club is just part of that. Tailor the project to what they can realistically get done.
- Be a reality check – young people don't have a huge amount of experience to call on and can be over optimistic about what they can achieve and what others will do for them.
- Publicise any achievements – it will help the young people keep motivated.

12. From positive activities...

- Risk assessments still need to be done and if you're doing anything off-site or hazardous, extra parental consent needs to be obtained.

12.3 Young people taking more responsibility in the youth club

This could be by running activities, helping out collecting subs or behind the coffee bar. You could make this happen by providing coaching or mentoring, or by training young people to become senior members and when they are old enough, volunteer youth workers. They can also help by providing information and guidance to the management committee at meetings, doing research or being part of a 'members' group', which provides a link between the management committee and the young people. See **Section 13 'Involving young people in decision making and volunteering'** for more information about this.

12.4 Involving young people in community action

Young people generally have ideas about how their communities can be better. Some aren't achievable (such as building a multiplex cinema in a small village) but some are (such as improving the recreation ground). Some ideas aren't even to do with young people but are for the benefit of the whole community, such as improving street lighting or increasing the number of litter bins. Young people can be enthusiastic and energetic fundraisers. The first step here is to involve adults from the decision making bodies in the community so the young people have access to adults with power. Your role is then to support the young people to work with these adults to achieve their goal. Research is often a first step. See **Section 13 'Involving young people in decision making and volunteering'** for more information about this.

12.5 Staff development and training

A lot can be done with young people if you have enthusiastic staff. Many people have skills that are transferable to youth work. For example, office workers have organisational skills, childcare workers are good at play and parents are experienced at dealing with young people. Many good youth clubs are run by volunteers with no formal training.

Training is a good idea, however. Somerset Youth and Community Service can provide courses for volunteers that are tailored to suit the needs of your youth clubs. Courses can include behaviour management, programme planning and developing senior members. Please contact SYCS on 01823 349852 for more information.

Some staff, however, want a better grounding in youth work theory and practice. Various courses are available for staff (paid and unpaid) to give them a basic grounding and possibly a nationally recognised qualification. For more information on youth work courses, contact Somerset Centre for Integrated Learning (SCIL) on 01823 368280 or visit the website www.scilearning.org.uk and click on 'Youth'. SCIL also runs training days that feature many different courses aimed at people working with young people. Called 'Interactive Training Days', attendance is often free or subsidised by Somerset Youth and Community Service. Sample programmes can be found at the SCIL website and include safeguarding, group work, conflict resolution and sexual health, among others.

If you want to find other specific courses please contact Somerset Youth and Community Service on 01823 349852 for information.

12.6 Other organisations that may be of help

Please refer to **Section 15 'Support from Somerset County Council and other organisations'** for information about other organisations in Somerset that can be useful, providing training, support, payroll services or opportunities for young people to get involved in things outside their local area.

Appendix 61 gives a list of websites that either give information useful when doing issue-based work with young people, or have information and advice for those involved in youth work, or downloadable resources that can be used in youth clubs with young people, or all three. When you have some spare time, have a look around.

13. Involving young people in decision making and volunteering

It is a good idea to involve the young people in decision making about your youth club wherever you can – after all, they are the experts on being young people and you are trying to provide the best club for them that you can! Also, many young people are happy to help out with things. Some young people really benefit from being given the extra responsibility that young helpers (or young volunteers or senior members as they are sometimes called) have.

13.1 Involving young people in decision making in a 'positive activities' youth club

There are lots of ways to involve young people. If you are providing a positive activity youth club, young people's involvement will probably be limited to helping to set the ground rules, having ideas about the programme (if you have one) or what to stock in the tuck shop. Young people may also help staff run some activities.

13.2 Involving young people in decision making in a 'youth work' youth club

If you are looking to provide youth work, there are lots of ways to further involve young people. In **Section 11 'Running your youth club'**, enabling young people to have a say in the programme and setting ground rules with young people have already been mentioned.

You can further involve young people in other ways too – for example:

- Helping to run the coffee bar
- Getting the views of all youth club members on certain issues
- Being in a members' committee
- Welcoming new members to the club
- Identifying the needs of young people
- Fundraising
- Assisting the youth worker with activities and planning
- Helping to organise events and activities
- Volunteering at the Junior Club (if you have one)

- Encouraging other young people to join in
- Working with young people with special needs
- Choosing new furniture and equipment
- Collecting subs on the door
- Appointing youth workers
- Encouraging other young people to take on more responsibility and mentoring them
- Representing young people (for example: on the management committee, in parish/town/district council meetings)
- Planning and carrying out special projects (for example: a skateboard park, graffiti wall, open day, fashion show, decoration of the club)
- Many other things!

For many of these activities, young people can be supported to take more responsibility on an *ad hoc* basis – with staff supervising and coaching them. However, you or your young people may like to have a more structured approach to taking on more responsibility and might like some training. Somerset Youth and Community Service may be able to help you to achieve this – there are training resources aimed at enabling young people to take more responsibility called the 'Activ8rs' programme. This consists of a six week course, or stand alone workshops (complete with notes, handouts and exercises), designed to be delivered by staff (paid and unpaid) to young people. Please contact SYCS on 01823 349852 for more information about this.

13.3 Young people's members' groups

It is good to have a group of young people happy to advise the management committee on the running of the youth club and/or to carry out projects themselves. The remit of the members' group can be as big or small as is appropriate for the club, and the young people involved. It is important that all members have a say in the running of their club if they choose to. Therefore when setting up the group, try to make it as representative of the young people attending as possible. Some clubs hold elections! The group will need help and support from an enthusiastic staff member who is good at enabling others to achieve, rather than doing it all themselves.

Things a members' group could get involved in include:

- Guiding the management committee on decisions about the running of the club and attending management committee meetings
- Running and stocking the coffee bar
- Interviewing staff

SOMERSET County Council

- Organising fundraising events
- Undertaking surveys or research on what people want
- Suggest and revise rules for the club
- Enthuse other young people to be involved
- Discourage destructive behaviour
- Organise special events and activities
- Encourage and promote consultation about major decisions
- Liaise with the local community to improve the profile of the club and the young people
- Helping to publicise the club

It is very similar to being a senior member, but the key role is helping the management committee make decisions and make the club run more smoothly. It is also a group, rather than an individual activity.

There are some pitfalls to beware of, such as the members' group becoming elitist and blocking other young people's participation. To avoid this, keep other youth club members informed about what the members' group is doing (even when you are not sure how interested they are!) by getting the members' group to chat to them, meet them or by designing posters. Also, always keep the door open for new members!

Another benefit to having a members' group is the writing of funding bids. It is increasingly common for funders to expect young people's direct input to any bid that is submitted.

When/if your members' group (or representatives from that group) attend management committee meetings, it's best to put some time aside before each meeting to tell them about the group/committee, talk them through any papers and brief them about their role. It's also good to prepare the adult group/committee, to ensure that they listen to the young people and don't confuse them with jargon. Sometimes it's appropriate (particularly at the start) to have young people at the meetings for specific agenda items only, as it can be boring for them.

How the members' group is chosen is up to you – but it's best to ask the young people for their views first. Sometimes there is a limited number of young people who are interested, so they can just become the members' group. Sometimes there are too many young people and so having a club election is the best way forward. This could involve members nominating themselves, doing a two minute speech about why they should be elected and then having a club vote – conducted anonymously of course. If a members' group becomes a long-term working group, elections are very important – otherwise the group could become elitist and actually decrease young people's involvement (by excluding some young people) rather than increasing it.

Be sure to reward the young people who are part of your members' group – certificates and trips out are good rewards, as is recognising their voluntary effort at meetings and in the press. Young people will also learn key skills such as planning, organising, team work and communication. Publicise these benefits when recruiting to your members' group and it will help encourage more young people to join.

For many of these members' group activities, young people can be supported on an *ad hoc* basis. To sustain a members' group, however, they need to meet regularly to hold their interest. Members' groups do benefit from training. Somerset Youth and Community Service may be able to help you achieve this – there are training resources aimed at enabling developing members' groups as part of the 'Activ8rs' programme. These are also designed to be delivered by staff (paid and unpaid) to young people. Please contact SYCS on 01823 349852 for more information about this.

13.4 Young people and staff interviews

Even if you haven't got senior members, Activ8rs or a members' group, you can still involve young people in staff appointments, whether the staff are paid or unpaid. You can do this directly by:

- Having a separate young people's panel when interviewing staff
- Having one or two young people on an adult interview panel
- Asking candidates to do an exercise (for example designing a poster) with the young people and asking young people for feedback

You can do it indirectly by:

- Asking young people to design their ideal staff member and using this as a template to measure against when interviewing
- Having a say when you're writing the job description
- Writing interview questions for adults to ask, along with what they'd like to see in the answers and using the questions in the interview

Young people's views need to be taken seriously in any interviews as they are the 'consumers'. Make sure that young people understand the need for confidentiality when being involved in staff interviews.

13.5 Young people and community action

Some youth clubs in towns and villages host the local youth parish/town council. This is usually a group of interested young people who work with an adult from the parish/town council to give young people a voice in local issues. Activities include:

- Taking part in (or conducting) consultations
- Taking part in (or conducting) research
- Campaigning and fundraising for specific village/town projects
- Having a voice in writing the community plan
- Carrying out projects (e.g. litter picks, designing recreational spaces, attending the poppy day parade, having a stall at local fairs etc.)
- Attending parish/town council meetings
- Making presentations about the needs of young people in the town/village

Generally, the young people involved need support and mentoring (as they don't know how to go about getting things done and the intricacies of village/town politics) and sometimes training. An interested community leader and an enthusiastic youth worker can make a huge difference to these groups and also the life of the town/village.

In terms of who makes up a youth town/parish council, the same guidance applies here as applies to members' groups (see above).

Somerset Youth and Community Service may be able to help you with this – there are training resources aimed at enabling young people to form youth councils. Please contact SYCS on 01823 349852 for more information about this.

13.6 And Finally...

Developing young people's skills to enable them to take more responsibility can be intense and hard work, as well as exciting and rewarding. It is good to remember that many of today's youth workers were yesterday's senior members or young volunteers – investing in these young people's development is a way of growing your own future youth workers and community leaders.

14. Ensuring quality

Whether you are delivering a positive activity or youth work, you will want to ensure that you are delivering a good quality service to young people. Having appropriate policies in place can help, as can having skilled and enthusiastic volunteers. However, you also need something to measure your service against.

14.1 Quality standards

In order to ensure that yours is a good quality youth club, you need to be clear about what you are trying to achieve and to what standard. Below is a list of quality standards that you might choose to use, along with some different ways of measuring them:

Positive Activity Standard	Youth Work Standard	Quality Standard	How to monitor and measure
✓	✓	Number of young people attending (set a target)	• Signing-in sheet
✓	✓	The venue is warm, well-lit and welcoming	• Observation • Young people's views
✓	✓	How often the club is open (set a target)	• Session sheets • Youth workers' reports
✓	✓	The young people enjoy the club	• Young people's views • Observation • Signing-in sheets (giving numbers attending)
✓	✓	Behaviour is of a good standard	• Youth workers' reports • Amount of damage/loss • Observation • Young people's views
✓	✓	The club is safe	• Number of accidents/incidents • Risk assessments in use • Observation • First aid, safeguarding, health and safety training undertaken
✓	✓	The programme is varied and interesting	• Programme posters • Young people's views

✓	✓	Staff have good relationships with young people	• Discussion with staff member in charge • Young people's views • Observation
✗	✓	Good information and advice is on offer	• Staff are trained • Observation that posters and leaflets are up to date and easily accessible • Young people's views
✗	✓	Young people learn and achieve	• Session sheets • Discussion with staff member in charge • Youth workers' reports • Observation • Young people's views • Number of local certificates given • Number of accredited certificates achieved
✗	✓	Young people are involved in decision making	• Number of young people who attend the management committee • Discussion with staff member in charge • Young people's views • Youth workers' reports

14.2 Monitoring visits

As you can see from the list of how to monitor your quality standards, it is good to visit the club to see for yourself. Whilst you're there, having an informal chat with young people is often the best way to get their views and ideas about what the club is like and how it can be improved. Please see **Appendix 56** for a sample visit monitoring sheet that you can use for all aspects of a visit. The form is designed for youth work, but can be adapted to positive activities by cutting things out (see the above table for a guide). Visiting once a year is enough, but visiting once a term is better, because the young people will get to know you and you can show that you listen to their views by making any changes needed.

14.3 Questionnaires

It is also good practice to ask young people's views using questionnaires, as they may not feel able to criticise their club in a conversation with someone they don't know well. Using an anonymous questionnaire can be a useful tool. Also included in the **Appendices** is a sample 'Your club, your views' questionnaire, that

can be given to young people to find out how they see their youth club (please see **Appendix 62**). You can use this questionnaire once a year to gauge young people's views – twice a year is better. Collating the responses into a short report for the management committee is a good way of getting a large number of young people's views across. If you make changes as a result of the questionnaire, let the young people know. It makes them feel listened to and so are more likely to tell you what you want to know.

14.4 Certificates

Also mentioned in the table above are local certificates – it's good to give these to young people at the completion of a project (such as training to be a senior member, doing a chunk of fundraising, completing a dance project etc.). It makes young people feel they have really achieved something. Also mentioned are accredited certificates. These are usually given out by awarding bodies and involve an amount of paperwork and moderation. Somerset Youth and Community Service run the 'Endeavour Credits', the simplest of these accreditation methods. Endeavour Credits have been redesigned to enable local youth clubs to give these awards simply. Please contact Somerset Youth and Community Service on 01823 349852 for more information.

14.5 A year-round quality assurance process

Finally, a good quality assurance process over a year may look like this:

January	Supervision with staff member in charge.
February	Monitoring visit to the club.
March	Supervision with staff member in charge (feedback from monitoring visit, as well as usual agenda).
April	Management Committee Report detailing: • Number of young people attending and opening frequency • Number of certificates • Programme update (including behaviour information) • Information about damages • Future plans This should be written by the staff member in charge. Also, feedback from monitoring visit.
May	Supervision with staff member in charge.
June	Monitoring visit to club.
July	Supervision with staff member in charge (feedback from monitoring visit, as well as usual agenda).

August	Management Committee Report, written by the member of staff in charge, as detailed in April. Also, feedback from monitoring visit.
September	Supervision with staff member in charge.
October	'Your Club, Your Views' survey undertaken.
November	Supervision with staff member in charge.
December	AGM Management Committee Report, written by the member of staff in charge, as detailed in April but with a year's overview and the results of the 'Your Club, Your Views' survey added.

Following the process outlined above will mean that you always know what is happening in the youth club and, importantly, the quality of what is being delivered to young people.

15. Support from Somerset County Council and other organisations

There is support for voluntary clubs out there, if you want it.

15.1 Somerset County Council

Somerset County Council is keen to help local groups, communities and volunteers start and sustain youth clubs and projects, and has produced this guide as part of that support. Advice and information is available from Somerset Youth and Community Service staff to help you work though the steps in the handbook, and we can often provide training for volunteers to help them understand the various roles that are required in a successful youth club or project. Sometimes we can even provide money!

For general enquiries, please use the following contact details:

Tel: 01823 349852
Email: Youthservice@somerset.gov.uk
Web: www.somersetyouth.co.uk

Somerset Youth and Community Service also runs the following, which may be of interest:

- **Youth Equipment Store**
The store has a stock of equipment that is useful for youth clubs; it includes camping and hiking kit, audio and visual equipment, games and even marquees! Also available is a range of equipment to help young disabled people. All equipment is available for hire at a reasonable cost. For a catalogue or more information, please visit the website: www.somersetyouth.co.uk, email: YES@somerset.gov.uk or call 01823 410131.

- **Minibus Hire**
Somerset Youth and Community Service has a small fleet of minibuses located across the county and available for hire by community groups. It also has a people carrier. For more information and to find out how to book the bus nearest you, please phone 01823 349852. Terms and conditions apply.

- **Duke of Edinburgh's Award Scheme**

Somerset Youth and Community Service supports the Duke of Edinburgh's Award scheme in schools, colleges and community groups across Somerset. If you are interested in running this at your youth club, appropriate training and support will be given. Please contact the Duke of Edinburgh's Award Scheme Co-ordinator on 08123 349855 or DofE@somerset.gov.uk.

- **Endeavour Credits**

This is an entry level accreditation scheme, designed to recognise young people's achievements in youth clubs. The scheme is simple and easy to use. For more information, please ring 01823 349852.

Support to help you start a youth club or project is also available from a number of other sources. If you are linked to a church, most of the dioceses have people in place that can help, and national organisations like Young Farmers have support in place to help develop and support new groups.

15.2 Somerset Rural Youth Project (SRYP)

Somerset Rural Youth Project is a voluntary youth work charity working with young people aged 11-25 in rural Somerset. SRYP:

- Provides individual young people with advice and support
- Offers a wide range of volunteering opportunities
- Supports young people's involvement in their community
- Provides support packages to local youth clubs
- Provides access to and participation in positive activities

SRYP has a vision of a Somerset where rural young people feel a sense of belonging, a willingness to contribute and a future that is not limited by access to opportunities and services. They aim to engage and support young people living in rural areas in a range of social, economic, educational and recreational opportunities designed to encourage social inclusion and life-long learning.

Tel: 01278 722100
Email: admin@sryp.org.uk
Web: www.sryp.org.uk

15.3 Children & Young People's Partnership in Somerset (CHYPPS)

CHYPPS (Children and Young People's Partnership in Somerset) is a member charity that delivers support to organisations in the voluntary sector working with children and young people up to 25.

The members represent a broad range of organisations, such as uniform and faith groups; play and youth organisations; and parent support groups.

Tel: 01458 253433
Email: admin@chypps.org.uk
Web: www.chypps.org.uk

15.4 The Volunteer Network (formerly Somerset Youth Volunteering Network)

TVN is a charity that has been running since 1999 and works with volunteers and organisations involved in all aspects of volunteering to help place suitable volunteers in great placements and vice versa. TVN supports volunteers throughout their activities as well as putting on volunteering taster days for them. The main focus for TVN is to assist volunteers aged 16-25, although it works with all age ranges. Young people are supported to obtain accreditation through the v awards, which range from a 'vThank You' certificate right through to a 'vImpact' award which acknowledges community benefits from a young person's positive action

Tel: 01458 836130
Email: info@volunteernetwork.org.uk
Web: www.somersetyouth.org.uk

15.5 The Diocese of Bath & Wells

Services for children and young people are coordinated by the Diocesan Education Department. The department is based in the Old Deanery, Wells and has a team of professional staff dedicated to serving many thousands of children and young people across historic Somerset. They support the adults who work with young people, in parishes, deaneries, local ministry groups/teams and schools, colleges and universities. The scope of the work is considerable, involving many partnerships and a wide range of activities and services are provided by the team. There are also links to useful resources for schools and parishes.

Tel: 01749 670777
Email: tony.cook@bathwells.anglican.org
Web: www.bathandwells.org.uk

15.6 Elim Church

The Elim Pentecostal Church is a growing movement of more than 550 Christian congregations in the UK and Ireland. Elim's 21st-

15. Support from SCC…

century churches seek to be a place of spiritual resource within their communities. The founders wanted the name of their new movement to express their vision and values, and so chose 'Elim', the name of an oasis in the Bible that the people of Israel discovered as they wandered through the desert.

Elim Pentecostal Church, Yeovil
Tel: 01935 429 214
Email: elim4yeovil@tiscali.co.uk
Web: www.elim4yeovil.com

Elim Connect Centre, Wells
Tel: 01749 677097
Email: info@connect-centre.org.uk
Web: www.connect-centre.org.uk

15.7 Somerset Federation of Young Farmers' Clubs

There are 25 Young Farmers' clubs in Somerset, grouped in five areas: Fosse, Sedgemoor, Severn, Wessex and West, each representing a 'corner' of Somerset. Young Farmers' clubs are run by the members for the members. Each club has advisory support and club leaders but their programme of events for the year is decided by the members. The County Office can help with whatever clubs need help with – as well as ensuring that child protection policies, health & safety risk assessments etc. are carried out to minimise threat or danger to all involved.

Tel: 01278 691711
Email: admin@somersetyfc.org.uk
Web: www.somersetyfc.org.uk

15.8 ViSTA Project

ViSTA is a learning and development charity working with individuals, communities and organisations to deliver learning opportunities, volunteer programmes and workforce development training.

Tel: 08453 580372
Email: admin@vistaproject.org.uk
Web: www.vistaproject.org.uk

Community Youth Club Handbook

Appendices

The samples contained within these appendices contain guidance notes which should not feature in the finished document and are for your reference only, these are italics in curly brackets {...}.

Text within angled brackets <...> indicate where you need to insert information.

Admin aide-mémoire

- Subscriptions log/signing-in sheet*

- Consent forms* in a membership file (including spare sheets)

- Session sheet file*

- Tuck book (to know when you need to re-order) and tuck sheet*

- Inventory

- Cash book

- Incidents and accidents sheets and file*

- Communications book

- Calendar (to record events due to take place)

- Scrapbook (to record all that the club has done)

- Health and safety file (including risk assessments*, health and safety calendar*, records of safety inspections etc.)

*There are samples of these in this pack.

Child Protection Policy Statement

<Name of Organisation> is committed to creating and maintaining the safest possible environment for children and young people.

We do this by:

- Recognising that all children and young people have the right to be free from abuse.

- Ensuring that all our staff and volunteers are carefully selected and accept responsibility for helping to prevent the abuse of children and young people in their care.

- Responding swiftly and appropriately to all suspicions or allegations of abuse and providing parents and children and young people with the opportunity to voice concerns.

- Appointing child protection officers who will take specific responsibility for child protection and act as the main point of contact for parents, children and outside agencies. Our child protection officers will be DBS (Disclosure and Barring Service) checked.

- Ensuring access to confidential information is restricted to the child protection officers or the appropriate external authorities.

- Reviewing the effectiveness of our Child Protection Policy and activities on a regular basis (at least annually at our AGM).

- Providing children and young people with a Child-Safe booklet containing guidelines on how the club will keep them safe.

- Introducing new members to the Child-Safe scheme.

Our child protection officers are:

_____   (Management Committee Member)

_____   (Staff Member)

Signed: ……………………………….. ………………………………….

                                                     (Block capitals)

Date: ………………………………….

Review date: ………………………………….

{N.B. This could be combined with the Staff Vetting Policy into a Safeguarding Policy.}

Code of Conduct Sample
For adults working with young people

Introduction

This code of conduct outlines the behaviour expected of **<Name of Organisation>**'s staff (paid or unpaid) and any helpers or staff from other organisations who engage with children and young people through **<Name of Organisation>**.

Purpose

This code has been developed to provide advice which will not only help to protect children, but will also help identify any practices which could be mistakenly interpreted and perhaps lead to false allegations of abuse being made against individuals.

Following this good practice code will also help to protect **<Name of Organisation>** by reducing the possibility of anyone using their role within the organisation to gain access to children in order to abuse them.

When working with children and young people for **<Name of Organisation>** all staff (paid or unpaid) are considered to be acting in a position of trust. It is therefore important that all staff are aware that they may be seen as role models by children and young people and must act in an appropriate manner at all times and follow the code of conduct.

All members of staff and volunteers are expected to report any breaches of this code to **<Name>**, in their role as Chair of the **<Name of Organisation>** Management Committee.

Staff who breach this code of conduct may be subject to disciplinary procedures.

Any breach of this code involving a member of staff from another agency may result in them being asked to leave the club. Serious breaches of this code may also result in a referral being made to a statutory agency such as the police or Children's Services Department.

When working with children and young people it is important to:

- always follow the **<Name of Organisation>** child protection policy
- listen to and respect children and young people at all times
- always avoid favouritism
- treat children and young people fairly and without prejudice
- value and take children and young people's contribution seriously

- always ensure equipment is used appropriately and for the purpose it was designed for
- ensure any contact with children and young people is appropriate and in relation to the work of the project
- always ensure language is appropriate and not offensive or discriminatory
- follow the ICT safety policy and report any breaches
- actively involve children and young people in planning activities wherever possible
- provide examples of good conduct you wish others to follow
- challenge unacceptable behaviour and report all allegations and suspicions of abuse

You must not:

- patronise or treat children and young people as if they are silly
- allow allegations to go unreported
- develop inappropriate relationships such as contact with young people that is not a part of the work of the youth club and agreed with the manager or leader. Sexual relationships between any adult member of staff and a child or young person using the youth club's services represent a serious breach of trust and are not permissible in any circumstances.
- let children and young people have your personal contact details (mobile number or address)
- use sarcasm or insensitive comments to children or young people
- act in a way that can be perceived as threatening or intrusive
- make inappropriate promises to children and young people, particularly in relation to confidentiality

The role of parents and carers

<Name of Organisation> welcomes and encourages parental involvement. Parents and carers are regarded as valuable partners in promoting positive behaviour and will be involved as appropriate. In the event of their child becoming the subject of behaviour sanctions, parents/carers will be informed and involved.

Issues of equality and individual needs will be addressed and supported in line with **<Name of Organisation>**'s Equalities Statement.

Two Sample Constitutions

Sample Constitution 1

Name: The name of the club shall be the _____ Club

Aim: The aim of the club is to help and educate young people aged 11-25 through their leisure time activities to develop their physical, mental and spiritual capacities, in order that they develop as individuals and members of society.

Management: The activities of the club shall be controlled by a Management Committee, which shall consist of:

a) the club leader(s) *ex officio*;
b) not less than 6 persons elected annually.

The Management Committee shall have the power to co-opt not more than 3 additional persons.

The Management Committee shall appoint a Chair, Secretary and Treasurer and such other officers, as deemed necessary.

The Management Committee shall meet at least 4 times a year.

The duties of the Management Committee shall be to devise methods for achieving the objects of the club and to exercise oversight of its activities and to see that the club's work is conducted in a safe and well organised manner.

The Management Committee may delegate powers to sub-committees. A sub-committee so formed shall in the exercise of powers so delegated conform to any regulations that may be imposed on it by the Management Committee.

Nominations for election to the Management Committee must be submitted in writing not less than 10 days before the Annual General Meeting.

Accounts: The Management Committee will ensure accurate accounts of all monies belonging to the club are kept and such accounts shall be audited annually and presented to the Annual General Meeting of the club.

Committee: General Meetings: A general meeting of the club's members, leaders and Management Committee shall be held once a year. Not less than 14 days' notice of the meeting shall be given.

The General Meeting shall receive an annual report and statement of accounts and shall elect the Management Committee for the forthcoming year.

© Somerset Youth and Community Service 2013

The Management Committee may convene a special General Meeting at any time. Not less than 14 days' notice of the meeting shall be given.

Young people's representation at the committee shall be ensured by a committee seat being dedicated to a club member, or an adult committee member being responsible for consulting club members.

Trustees: All properties and assets of the club shall be vested in the club's Trustees. All elected members of the committee, plus anyone appointed to the role, shall be Trustees.

Winding Up: In the event of the club being dissolved if, after the satisfaction of all debts and liabilities, there remains any property, this shall (subject to any existing agreements) be transferred to an organisation which shares the club's aim for young people to be used for similar charitable objectives in the area.

Constitution: This constitution shall only be altered by resolution passed by two-thirds majority of those present at a General Meeting. At least 14 days' notice is to be given of the proposed amendments.

Signed _____   Signed _____

                                Chair of Meeting   Secretary of Meeting

Date   _____

Sample Constitution 2

1. Name: The name of the club shall be _____

2. Objects: The object of the club is to promote the development of individuals through providing informal educational and leisure opportunities and by actively involving its members in the running of their club, community and society.

3. Powers: The club and its committee and trustees are empowered to:

a. Raise money for the benefit of the membership of the organisation;
b. Arrange all insurances as required;
c. Do all such lawful things as shall further the objects of the organisation.

4. Membership:

a. Membership of the club shall be open to young people aged 11-25.
b. All members shall have voting rights at the Annual General Meeting and Special General Meetings.

5. Resignation and Termination of Membership:

a. Any member may resign his/her membership by giving notice of resignation to the Secretary.
b. The Management Committee may terminate or suspend the membership of any member or volunteer if in its opinion his/her conduct is prejudicial to the interest of the organisation provided that the member or volunteer shall have the right of appeal.

6. Management Committee:

a. The Management Committee shall consist of the Chairperson, Treasurer, Secretary and up to 5 representatives of local people together with up to 4 young people who are members of the club.
b. The committee shall ensure accurate notes and minutes of meetings are kept.

7. Finance:

a. An account shall be opened in the name of the organisation with a bank or building society as agreed.
b. All cheques must be signed by not less than 2 of the organisation signatories.
c. The financial year shall be from April to March.
d. The Management Committee shall keep and audit proper accounts of all monies belonging to the club.
e. The accounts shall be presented to the Annual General Meeting.
f. All monies raised shall be used for the purposes of the Club except for the payment of out of pocket expenses incurred by members of the Management Committee or voluntary workers as agreed.

8. Annual General Meeting:

a. The Annual General Meeting shall be held during the month of June.
b. Not less than 14 days' notice of the meeting shall be given.
c. The business of the Annual General Meeting shall be:
   i. to receive the Annual Report of the Management Committee;
   ii. to receive the accounts of the organisation for the preceding financial year;
   iii. to elect the Management Committee in accordance with Clause 6.

9. Special Meetings:

a. Special meetings can be convened by 3 members of the Management Committee.
b. 14 days' notice must be given of such meeting.
c. The meeting may only consider the business specified on the notice.

10. Alterations to the constitution:

a. Any proposal to alter this constitution must be given in writing to the Secretary not less than 21 days before the date of the meeting at which it is to be considered.
b. Any alterations shall require the approval of a simple majority of the Management Committee present and voting at a General Meeting.

11. Dissolution:

a. If the Management Committee by a simple majority decides at any time that on the grounds of expenditure or otherwise, it is necessary to dissolve the organisation it should call a meeting of the members with the power to vote.
b. If such a decision is confirmed again by a simple majority of those present and voting at such a meeting, the Management Committee shall have the power to dispose of any assets after the settling of any debts, to a similar organisation or group serving young people in the area.

12. Adoption:

This Constitution was adopted at the first Management Committee meeting held on:

_____ at _____.

Signed: _____ Chair of Meeting

Signed: _____ Secretary of Meeting

Date: _____

Sample Drugs and Alcohol Policy

<Name of Organisation> recognises that some young people will have some involvement in drug and alcohol use. Whilst not condoning such use, we acknowledge that young people need information and advice to make informed choices. **<Name of Organisation>** must work within the law and provide a safe environment for all young people and staff. This policy covers illegal drugs, alcohol and volatile substances.

- Young people, staff and other building users are not allowed to bring illegal drugs or alcohol into our premises (this includes the building, surrounding areas and any vehicles).

- Staff will provide young people with accurate information and advice about drug use when appropriate. This may include referral to other organisations, giving leaflets and signposting to websites.

- If any young person or other user is found in possession of, or using, illegal drugs, alcohol or volatile substances, they will be asked to leave. If they do not leave, the police will be called and the incident reported. Personal safety of staff and young people is most important here and staff should only intervene if safe to do so. If in doubt, the police must be called.

- If staff find, or are handed, an illegal drug (or something they suspect to be an illegal drug), they can either dispose of it safely (by flushing down the toilet in front of another staff member) or take it to the police station for destruction (if the quantity of drug suggests supply). If taking to the police, the police must be informed before setting off that the staff member is coming in. Under no circumstances will staff hand any illegal substances back to a young person. All incidents must be recorded in the incident book.

- If staff are concerned that a young person may be supplying drugs on the premises, they will first discuss this with the young person. If they are still concerned that the young person is continuing to supply drugs, they will inform the police.

- Anyone under the influence of alcohol or drugs will not be allowed onto the premises. If the young person is unconscious, confused, disorientated, having trouble breathing or has taken a harmful toxic substance, this will be treated as a medical emergency. An ambulance will be called, first aid given and parents/carers informed. Immediately after the incident, staff will record the incident in the incident book and discuss with their line manager/Chair of the Management Committee.

- The **<Name of Organisation>** and its staff will co-operate with the police. This includes allowing access to the premises when needed. It does not include volunteering information about a young person's drug use as, apart from when there are safeguarding concerns, information given by young people is treated confidentially. However, staff will not actively obstruct the police or hamper a police enquiry as this can result in prosecution. Any queries must be discussed with the line manager/Chair of the Management Committee.

- Staff must not use any controlled or non-prescribed drug during working hours. Such use will be a serious disciplinary issue and may result in dismissal.

- This policy also applies when taking young people on day and residential trips.

Signed: _____ Date: _____

Chair of **<Name of Organisation>** Management Committee

Printed name: _____ Review date: _____

© Somerset Youth and Community Service 2013

Equalities Policy Sample

<Name of Organisation> is committed to creating a culture which promotes equality for children and young people. We recognise that discrimination is harmful to their well-being and development. We believe that children and young people may be discriminated against because of gender, race, disability, culture, religion, language, age, sexual orientation and HIV status.

We promote equality by:

- Creating a culture within our organisation where equality is at the core of all our activities.

- Working towards the elimination of discrimination and bullying, whether direct or indirect.

- Ensuring fairness, impartiality and consistency in all our working practices with young people.

- Setting and applying the highest in quality standards to ensure all children and young people have equality of opportunity.

- Ensuring all staff and volunteers are carefully selected and that they accept responsibility for helping to prevent discrimination against children in their care.

- Not treating all children and young people the same but striving to meet their particular needs.

The effectiveness of our Equalities Policy will be reviewed each year at the AGM with the Child Protection Policy.

Signed: Date:

On behalf of **<Name of Organisation>** Management Committee

First Aid Policy Sample

Staff (paid or unpaid) and young people will have ready access to adequate and appropriate first aid equipment and facilities at all times when they are at the club.

The Approved Code of Practice for First Aid suggests that in low-risk premises (such as the youth club) there should be one first aider for every 50 people with an additional first aider for every 100 people. **<Name of Organisation>** will abide by this. However, the number of staff and young people is not the only factor to take into account when determining the number of first aiders required and the number required may rise in certain circumstances (for example, where the activity is hazardous or the venue changes).

First aid boxes should not contain tablets, medication or pharmaceutical preparations. In all cases, volunteers must be informed of their location and they must be clearly identified in accordance with relevant Health and Safety Regulations, i.e. green background with a white cross.

The staff member in charge will check the contents of the first aid box at the beginning of each session, make a note of any items that need replenishing and purchase as necessary (to be reimbursed from youth club funds). Supplies in first aid boxes will be checked annually for expiry dates.

First aid treatments will only be administered by people who have completed an approved training course approved by the Health and Safety Executive (HSE) and relevant refresher training, i.e. every three years.

First aiders will be available at all times that staff and young people are at the club. Arrangements will be made to maintain cover for first aiders taking holidays.

The only exception to having a trained first aider is in very low-risk environments in which case there should be an 'appointed person' responsible for calling medical assistance and if he or she has been trained to do so, to administer emergency first aid.

First aiders will be provided with a formal system for recording incidents and accidents (incident book). Information to be recorded should include:

- Date and time of the incident
- The location
- The name of the injured person
- Details of the injury/illness and any first aid administered
- Subsequent actions (e.g. sent home, taken to hospital, went back to work)
- The details of the first aider or appointed person (name, signature, etc.)

First aid qualifications held by staff will be recorded as part of our management procedures.

Signed: Date:

On behalf of **<Name of Organisation>** Management Committee.

Guide to sources of youth funding

Somerset County Council Youth & Community Service manages three funding programmes for young people in the county:

Youth Bank

Grants of up to £350 to enable young people aged 11-19 years (up to 25 for young people with special needs) to take part in positive activities. Priority is to enable disadvantaged young people to access opportunities.

Children's Bank

Similar to Youth Bank but for children aged 8-11 years.

Youth & Community Group Grants

Grants of up to £5,000 to support community groups to create or sustain youth clubs or drop-in provision. Funding can also be used to train young people and/or adults as volunteers to run youth provision.

For more information about how to apply for these grants, please contact:

Youth & Community Service
Holway Centre
Taunton
Somerset
TA1 2JD

Email: youthservice@somerset.gov.uk

Tel: 01823 349852

or see the Youth Funding pages on
www.somersetyouth.co.uk

If the grants available via Somerset County Council do not meet your needs or if your application has been unsuccessful, you may find the information about other sources of funding in this booklet helpful.

Whilst we endeavour to ensure this information is correct and up to date this is not always possible. If you are aware of other appropriate funding that is not featured in this booklet or if you discover details that have changed, please let us know.

© Somerset Youth and Community Service 2013

Youth Funding Sources

Somerset Community Foundation

The foundation administers a variety of funds for grant making and will be able to advise on which grant programme fits your needs or recommend an alternative funder if the project falls outside the Community Foundation's criteria. Each of these funds is open to small voluntary and community groups that have a bank account, constitution and produce annual income and expenditure accounts. Applications are considered by an independent panel of local people with the skills, knowledge and experience to make decisions on awards.

Grant fund administered by Somerset Community Foundation include:

- Comic Relief
- Eagle House Trust
- Field House Trust
- David Price Fund
- Shoon Fund
- W.C.S. Pickford Trust
- Courage Family Fund
- Myakka Fund
- Angela Yeoman Fund
- Peter Wyman Fund
- Somerset Masonic Fund
- Team Somerset 500 Club Fund

- Sir John Wills Memorial Trust
- Grave Family Trust Fund
- John & Dorothy Ball Fund
- Party Packs Fund
- Summerfield & Tauntfield Fund
- McGreevy Charitable Trust
- West Somerset Relief Fund
- Christopher Tanner Memorial Trust
- Team Somerset Healthy Living Fund

Contact: Jocelyn Blacker (Grants & Finance Manager) or Karen Collins (Grants Administrator), Somerset Community Foundation, Yeoman House, The Royal Bath & West Showground, Shepton Mallet, Somerset, BA4 6QN

Tel: 01749 344949
Email: info@somersetcf.org.uk
Website: www.somersetcf.org.uk

Pople Charitable Trust

The scheme is intended to support charitable organisations undertaking projects in the fields of education, youth work and assisting the elderly.

Contact: Don Pople, Pople Charitable Trust, Avonhurst, 38 Church Road, Abbots Leigh, Bristol, BS8 3QP

Tel: 01275 374789

Co-operative Membership Community Fund

The fund offers grants of £100-£2,000 to community, voluntary, or self-help groups, community charities or local branches of national charities. Eligible groups must carry out positive work in the community and must:

- address a community issue
- ideally be innovative in its approach
- support co-operative values and principles
- provide a good long-term benefit to the community

Contact: Grants Administrator, Community Fund, 6th Floor, New Century House, Manchester, M60 4ES

Tel: 0844 262 4001
Email: community.fund@co-operative.coop
Website: www.co-operative.coop/membership/local-communities/community-fund

SITA Trust Enhancing Communities Programme

The Enhancing Communities Programme Core Fund is provided by SITA Trust through the Landfill Communities Fund. Landfill operators collect a tax for every tonne of waste that goes into their sites. A proportion of this tax can be allocated to the Landfill Communities Fund to support community and environmental improvement projects. SITA Trust receives its funding from the waste management company, SITA UK, which owns landfill sites across the UK.

The Core Fund provides funding for physical improvements to:

- Community facilities
- Historic buildings/structures
- Sport and recreation facilities

Contact: SITA Trust, The Coach House, Eastwood Park, Falfield, South Gloucestershire, GL12 8DA

Tel: 01454 262910
Email: info@sitatrust.org.uk
Website: www.sitatrust.org.uk

Hilden Charitable Trust

The Hilden Charitable Fund awards grants to projects in the UK and developing countries. The aim of the fund is to address disadvantage, notably by supporting causes that are less likely to raise funds from public subscriptions. Fund policy is directed largely at supporting work at community level.

Contact: Hilden Charitable Trust, 34 North End Road, London, W14 OSH

Tel: 0207 603 1525
Email: hildencharity@hotmail.com
Website: www.hildencharitablefund.org.uk

Eucalyptus Charitable Foundation

The Eucalyptus Charitable Foundation Grant is provided and administered by The Eucalyptus Charitable Foundation and is available for voluntary and community organisations in the UK.

The scheme is intended to support national charities and local organisations undertaking general charitable projects.

Contact: The Eucalyptus Charitable Foundation, c/o KPMG LLP, 100 Temple Street, Bristol, BS1 6AG

Tel: 0117 905 4000

Henry Smith Charity

The Henry Smith Charity awards revenue and capital activity grants for work in the UK. Priority is given to work with groups experiencing social and/or economic disadvantage. Grants can be made in the following categories:

- Black, Asian and Minority Ethnic (BAME)
- Carers
- Community Service
- Disability
- Domestic and Sexual Violence
- Drugs, Alcohol and Substance Misuse.
- Ex-Service Men and Women
- Family Services

- Healthcare
- Homelessness
- Lesbian, Gay, Bisexual and Transgender
- Mental Health
- Older People
- Prisoners and Ex-offenders
- Prostitution and Trafficking
- Refugees and Asylum Seekers Young People

Contact: The Henry Smith Charity, 6th Floor, 65 Leadenhall Street, London, EC3A 2AD

Tel: 020 7264 4970
Website: www.henrysmithcharity.org.uk

Somerset Crimebeat

Somerset Crimebeat aims to give young people up to the age of 25 an opportunity to help combat crime and the causes of crime in the community. To be eligible for a grant, your project should:

- allow young people to tackle the problems of their community themselves
- have sufficient adult and professional support
- concentrate on issues of crime prevention and community safety
- promote young people as valued members of the community they take a positive role in
- include as many sections of the community as possible
- empower young people with confidence and a sense of achievement

Contact: Simon Paul Selby, Co-ordinator, c/o Radstock Police Station, Wells Road, Radstock, BA3 3SG

Tel: 07768 598106
Email: sps.rb@tesco.net
Website: www.somersetcrimebeat.org

The Nominet Trust

nominettrust

The Nominet Trust aims to bring together and invest in people committed to using the internet to make society better and take action for social good. To achieve the greatest impact, the focus is on supporting projects and organisations that use digital technology to improve the lives of the disadvantaged and vulnerable and to strengthen communities. The trust aims to seek out, galvanise and support innovative projects that use digital technology to design radically new solutions to address specific social challenges.

Contact: Nominet Trust, Minerva House, Edmund Halley Road, Oxford Science Park, Oxford OX4 4DQ

Tel: 01865 334000
Email: enquiries@nominettrust.org.uk
Website: www.nominettrust.org.uk

Young Roots (Heritage Lottery Fund) heritage lottery fund

Young Roots aims to engage young people aged 11-25 with their heritage. It funds projects that stem directly from the interest and ideas of young people, who are supported by youth and heritage organisations to develop skills, build confidence, and connect with their local communities. To receive a Young Roots grant, your project must relate to the varied heritage of the UK and:

- provide new opportunities for a wider range of young people to learn about their own and others' heritage
- allow young people to lead and take part in creative and engaging activities
- develop partnerships between youth organisations and heritage organisations and
- create opportunities to celebrate young people's achievements in the project and share their learning with the wider community

Your project must also create new opportunities for young people to either volunteer in heritage or gain skills in identifying, recording, interpreting or caring for heritage.

Contact: Heritage Lottery Fund, 7 Holbein Place, London, SW1W 8NR

Tel: 020 7591 6042
     020 7591 6044
Email: enquire@hlf.org.uk
Website: www.hlf.org.uk

Wingate Foundation

The Harold Hyam Wingate Foundation considers applications for grants from small charitable organisations, but does not fund individuals. The Foundation supports six specific categories:

- Jewish life & learning
- Performing arts
- Music
- Education & social exclusion
- Developing countries
- Medical research travel grants

Contact: 20-22 Stukeley Street, London, WC2B 5LR

Website: www.wingatefoundation.org.uk

Money Advice Trust – Innovation Grants

Money Advice Trust

MAT supports agencies to provide free, independent, effective advice to clients on the strategies available to help them deal with their debts and financial circumstances. Projects must be innovative and look for new approaches to an old issue or the use of an established approach for new issues, needs or audiences. The priority areas are:

- Developing new information, resources and ways of delivering advice that can be shared with others, and replicated widely.
- Projects that combine money advice and financial capability for people who are usually excluded from society.
- Work that will assist those who are homeless or facing homelessness.

Contact: Emily Hopkins, Money Advice Trust, 21 Garlick Hill, London, EC4V 2AU

Tel: 020 7653 9734
Email: grants@moneyadvicetrust.org
Website: www.moneyadvicetrust.org/content.asp?ssid=121

Breaks 4 Kids – Youth Hostel Association

Breaks 4 Kids is a charitable fund founded and supported by the YHA. It helps to fund youth group and school trips for children from low income households, by contributing up to 50% of the cost of their YHA accommodation and food. This gives children who would otherwise be left behind the chance to be included in the trip. Applications must be made at least 8 weeks before the trip commences.

Contact: YHA, Trevelyan House, Dimple Road, Matlock, Derbyshire, DE4 3YH

Tel: 01629 592700
Email: customerservices@yha.org.uk
Website: www.breaks4kids.co.uk

Esmée Fairbairn Foundation

The Esmée Fairbairn Foundation aims to improve quality of life throughout the UK by funding the charitable work of organisations with the ideas and ability to achieve positive change. It often supports work that might otherwise be considered difficult to fund, responding to need and being willing to take risks on work that breaks new ground, deals with challenging and difficult issues, or needs a more unusual form of financial help such as a loan.

The foundation encourages enterprising people and projects, preferring to support work that is sustainable and responsibly planned. The main sectors supported are:

- Arts
- Education and Learning
- Environment
- Social Change

Contact: Esmée Fairbairn Foundation, Kings Place, 90 York Way, London, N1 9AG

Tel: 020 7812 3700
Email: info@esmeefairbairn.org.uk
Website: www.esmeefairbairn.org.uk

Trusthouse Charitable Foundation

Trusthouse Charitable Foundation's grants programme supports projects in the UK that address issues in rural communities and/or areas of urban deprivation.

Within these two main headings, they are interested in helping established projects that work in the fields of Community Support; Arts, Education & Heritage; Disability & Health Care.

Contact: Trusthouse Charitable Foundation, 65 Leadenhall Street, London, EC3A 2AD

Tel: 020 7264 4990
Website: www.trusthousecharitablefoundation.org.uk

Lloyds TSB Foundation

The foundation funds charities working to tackle disadvantage across England and Wales. The focus is on supporting underfunded charities that make a significant difference to the lives of disadvantaged people by helping them to play a fuller role in the community.

The foundation funds charities to continue and develop existing community-based work, or to develop the organisation or its services. For example, funding has been allocated to:

- Enable the continued provision of services;
- Support the expansion of services;
- Help improve the quality of services;
- Maintain and or improve capacity or effectiveness;
- Encourage learning and best practice;
- Lobby or campaign at a local, regional or national level.

Grants of one to three years that are appropriate to the size and needs of each charity can be awarded.

Contact: Lloyds TSB Foundation, Pentagon House, 52-54 Southwark Street, London SE1 1UN

Tel: 0870 411 1223
Email: enquiries@lloydstsbfoundations.org.uk
Website: www.lloydstsbfoundations.org.uk

Norman Family Charitable Trust

The Norman Family Charitable Trust
Charity Number 277616

The Trust funds good causes in Devon, Somerset and Cornwall or national charities carrying out work that will benefit these areas. The scheme is open for any charitable purposes and generally offers awards of up to £5,000.

Contact: 14 Fore Street, Budleigh Salterton, Devon, EX9 6NG

Tel: 01395 446699
Website: www.nfct.org

Peter Harrison Foundation

The foundation supports those charitable activities that demonstrate an existing high level of voluntary commitment, together with well-planned and thought-out projects. The key areas supported are:

- opportunities through sport
- special needs and care for children and young people
- opportunities through education

However, other projects may be funded at the trustees' discretion.

Contact: Peter Harrison Foundation, Foundation House, 42-48 London Road, Reigate, Surrey, RH2 9QQ

Tel: 01737 228000
Email: enquiries@peterharrisonfoundation.org
Website: www.peterharrisonfoundation.org

The Skinners' Company Lady Neville Charity

The charity provides grants to make a clear and significant contribution to grassroots charitable organisations working in designated priority areas. One-off grants of up to £1,000 are made to small registered charities and not-for-profit organisations. The priority areas are:

- Local Heritage – helping local groups conserve and restore their landmarks, landscape, traditions and culture.
- Performing and Visual Arts – undertaking a particular activity in any field in this area.

Contact: The Grants Administrator, Skinners' Hall, 8 Dowgate Hill, London, EC4R 2SP

Tel: 020 7213 0562
Email: charitiesadmin@skinners.org.uk
Website: www.skinnershall.co.uk/charities/lady-neville-charity.htm

Sylvia Waddilove Foundation

The foundation awards grants of £1,000-£10,000 to registered charities in the UK for work in:

- Education
- The visual and performing arts
- Medical research
- The relief of disability and severe illness
- The accommodation of those in need
- The skills-based training of young people
- The preservation of buildings of architectural and historical significance

Contact: Pothecary Witham Weld Solicitors, 70 St George's Square, London, SW1V 3RD

Tel: 0207 821 8211
Email: waddilove@pwwsolicitors.co.uk
Website: www.pwwsolicitors.co.uk/charitable-applications/charity-details/the-sylvia-waddilove-foundation-uk

Peter Hamlyn Foundation

The Paul Hamlyn Foundation is one of the larger independent grant-making foundations in the UK. They make grants to organisations which aim to maximise opportunities for individuals to experience a full quality of life, both now and in the future. In particular they are concerned with children and young people, and others who are disadvantaged. The Foundation prefers to support work that others may find hard to fund, perhaps because it breaks new ground, is too risky or is unpopular.

Contact: 5-11 Leeke Street, London, WC1X 9HY

Tel: 020 7812 3300
Email: information@phf.org.uk
Website: www.phf.org.uk

Santander Foundation

The Santander Foundation has two grant programmes to help disadvantaged people in the UK:

- Santander Community Plus – grants of up to £5,000 for salaries, equipment or materials.
- Central Grants Programme – provides grants of up to £10,000 to improve education & training or financial capability.

Applications can only be accepted from UK registered charities.
Contact: Alan Eagle, Santander Foundation, 201 Grafton Gate East, Milton Keynes, MK9 1AN

Email: grants@santander.co.uk
Website: www.santanderfoundation.org.uk

Prince's Countryside Fund

The Prince's Countryside Fund seeks to address and provide funding to tackle five key issues:

- Rural isolation
- Decline of rural communities
- Low farming incomes
- Lack of access to training
- Disconnection with the value of the countryside

To be eligible for a grant you will need to demonstrate that your project is tackling at least one of the five issues.

The fund aims to address these issues by providing grants that will:

- Improve service provision in rural areas
- Support rural enterprise
- Support farming businesses
- Provide training opportunities for young people
- Educate people about the value of the countryside

Contact: Victoria Elms, Business in the Community, 137 Shepherdess Walk, London, N1 7RQ

Email: PCFapplication@bitc.org.uk
Website: www.princescountrysidefund.org.uk

Leonard Laity Stoate Charitable Trust

THE LEONARD LAITY STOATE CHARITABLE TRUST

This charitable fund makes grants to other charities and voluntary organisations in England and Wales, with a clear preference for the West of England. Grants of £100-£2,000 are available. The scheme primarily supports projects with the following themes:

- Medical welfare and disability
- Children and young people
- The environment
- The disadvantaged
- Community projects
- Methodism and other churches

Contact: The Leonard Laity Stoate Charitable Trust, 7 Sherwood Close, Bracknell, Berkshire, RG12 2SB

Website: www.stoate-charity.org.uk

UnLtd Awards

UnLtd*

UnLtd's Millennium Awards offer a complete package of support to provide practical and financial support to social entrepreneurs in the UK, offering encouragement and support, contact with others just like them and access to training to give their projects the best chance of success. UnLtd awards are only available for individuals. The are three levels of award:

- **Try it awards**: up to £500 to allow people to test their ideas.
- **Do it awards**: up to £5,000 to get the project up & running, backed by development support.
- **Build it awards**: up to £15,000 to enable the social entrepreneur to work full time on their venture, backed by more intensive development support and networking.

Contact: UnLtd Awards Head Office, 123 Whitecross Street, Islington, London, EC1Y 8JJ

Tel: 0207 566 1100
Website: www.unltd.org.uk

Prince's Trust Community Cash Awards

Community Cash Awards are grants of up to £3,000 to help set up projects that will benefit the community. Successful applicants also receive support to help plan their project, research their budget, set goals and learn about the community.

Applications are accepted from those who are either:

- aged 14-16, and not expected to achieve 5 GCSEs grades A* - C; or
- aged 16-25 and not in education, training or work (or working less than 16 hours a week).

Projects must be run and managed by young people, benefit the local community and help the people running the project develop new skills for the future. The funding cannot be used for expeditions or overseas travel, fundraising activities for charity; trips and outings (unless they have educational value), or for spreading religious or political views.

Contact: The Prince's Trust South West Regional Office, 9 Marsh Street, Bristol, BS1 4AA

Tel: 0117 9292 300
Email: webinfosw@princes-trust.org.uk
Website: www.princes-trust.org.uk/need_help/grants.aspx

Viridor Credits

Viridor Credits provide capital funding for new projects by not-for-profit groups. Eligible projects include:

- Provision or maintenance of public amenities.
- Projects to enhance the biological diversity of a species or habitat.
- Maintenance, restoration or renovation of public buildings of historical or architectural interest.

Contact: Viridor Credits, Aintree House, Blackbrook Park Avenue, Taunton, Somerset, TA1 2PX

Tel: 01823 624656
Email: enquiries@viridor-credits.co.uk
Website: www.viridor-credits.co.uk

Wessex Watermark Awards

The Watermark Award is an environmental grant scheme that has offered funding for projects in the region since 1993. It enables groups, schools, councils and other organisations to apply for financial help when carrying out projects. Organised by the Conservation Foundation, all applications are considered by a panel of experts chaired by botanist and TV presenter David Bellamy. Grants of £100 to £1,500 are awarded quarterly to schemes that aim to improve, preserve or conserve the local environment. A Watermark Gold Award worth £2,500 is available if a special project has been singled out by the judges.

Contact: Public Relations, Wessex Water, Claverton Down, Bath BA2 7WW

Tel: 01225 526327
Email: info@wessexwater.co.uk
Website: www.wessexwater.co.uk

Sport England – Protecting Playing Fields

Sport England's funding programme, Protecting Playing Fields is part of the Places People Play Olympic legacy mass participation programme. It is investing £10 million of National Lottery funding in community sports projects via five funding rounds over three years from 2011-2014.

Eligible organisations are those entitled to receive public funding including:

- Voluntary or community organisations
- Local authorities
- Sports clubs
- Playing field associations
- Charities
- Education establishments

Contact: Sport England, 3rd Floor Victoria House, Bloomsbury Square, London, WC1B 4SE

Tel: 08458 508 508
Email: funding@sportengland.org
Website: www.sportengland.org/funding/protecting_playing_fields.aspx

sported.

Sported is a charity established to support organisations that use sport as a tool to engage with disadvantaged young people. Membership to **sported.** is free, and once you are a member you have the opportunity to access funding, project support, help with financial planning and funding applications. Membership is accepted from any organisation or community group that uses sport as the tool for development of young people (11-25 years) who would be classed as deprived (whether that be rurally, socially, economically or through disability).

Contact: sported., 20 St James's Street, London, SW1A 1ES

Tel: 020 7389 1905
Email: info@sported.org.uk
Website: www.sported.org.uk

Adam Stansfield Foundation

The foundation promotes community participation in healthy recreation for the benefit of children and young people up to the age of 16, residing in Devon, Herefordshire and Somerset by the provision of grants and facilities for playing football.

Contact: The Adam Stansfield Foundation, PO Box 174, Tiverton, Devon, EX16 0ET

Email: enquiries@adamstansfieldfoundation.com
Website: www.adamstansfieldfoundation.com

Football Foundation

The Football Foundation is funded by the Premier League, the Football Association and the government to direct £30 million every year into grass roots sport. It aims to improve facilities, create opportunities and build communities throughout England.

The Football Foundation has a range of schemes available, including:

- Grass Roots Facilities Fund
- Build the Game
- Football Stadia Improvement Fund
- Fan's Fund
- Premier League Community Facility Fund
- Mayor of London
- Extra Time
- Grow the Game

Contact: The Football Foundation, Whittington House, 19-30 Alfred Place, London, WC1E 7EA

Tel: 0845 345 4555
Email: enquiries@footballfoundation.org.uk
Website: www.footballfoundation.org.uk

Sportsmatch

Sportsmatch makes awards to not-for-profit organisations that have secured sponsorship to deliver new community projects for young people (14+) and adults to take up and keep a sporting habit for life. Awards of between £1,000 and £100,000 can be made to match funding from no more than five sponsors, with each sponsor contributing a minimum of £1,000.

Contact: 3rd Floor Victoria House, Bloomsbury Square, London, WC1B 4SE

Tel: 08458 508 508
Email: info@sportengland.org
Website: www.sportengland.org/funding/sportsmatch.aspx

LankellyChase Foundation

LankellyChase Foundation works to bring about change that will transform the quality of life of people who face severe and multiple disadvantages. The focus is particularly on the clustering of serious social harms, such as homelessness, substance misuse, mental illness, poverty and crime and victimisation.

Contact: 1 The Court, High Street, Harwell, Didcot, Oxfordshire, OX11 0EY

Tel: 01235 820044
Email: enquiries@lankellychase.org.uk
Website: www.lankellychase.org.uk

Cable & Wireless Worldwide Foundation

Grants of up to £10,000 are available to not-for-profit organisations in the UK that support, research, develop or implement specialist communication requirements for those with special needs.

Contact: Tracy O'Brien (Head of Corporate Responsibility & Chairman), Worldwide House, Western Road, Bracknell, Berkshire, RG12 1RW

Email: Foundation@cw.com
Website: www.cw.com/about-us/cww-foundation

Family Fund

Family Fund aims to ease the additional pressures faced by families who are raising a disabled child or young person with additional complex needs or a serious illness. The fund can help with essential items such as washing machines, fridges and clothing but can also consider grants for sensory toys, computers and much needed family breaks together.

Contact: 4 Alpha Court, Monks Cross Drive, York, YO32 9WN

Tel: 08449 744 099
Email: info@familyfund.org.uk
Website: www.familyfund.org.uk

Baily Thomas Charitable Fund

The Baily Thomas
Charitable Fund

The Baily Thomas Charitable Fund supports
voluntary organisations working in the field of learning disability. It considers learning disability to cover the conditions generally referred to as severe learning difficulties, together with autism. Funding is available for projects concerning children or adults. Funding is available to aid the care and relief of those affected by learning disability.

Application deadlines for General Grants are 1 May or 1 October each year. Applications for Small Grants can be made at any time. Applications will only be considered from voluntary organisations that are registered charities or are associated with a registered charity.

Contact: Mrs Ann Cooper, Baily Thomas Charitable Fund, c/o TMF
          Management UK Ltd, 400 Capability Green, Luton, Beds, LU1 3AE

Tel: 01582 439225
Email: info@bailythomas.org.uk
Website: www.bailythomas.org.uk

Speak Up Film Fund

The Speak Up Fund is provided and administered by the Community Film Unit. Funding supports voluntary organisations across England for film-based projects that show dedication to their local communities. Grants are for 20% to 50% of project costs.

Contact: Community Film Unit, Leacroft Youth Centre, Leacroft Road,
          Staines, Middlesex, TW18 4PB

Tel: 01784 469 751
Email: speakupfund@communityfilmunit.co.uk
Website: www.communityfilmunit.co.uk/fund.html

Awards for Young Musicians

The charity supports the UK's most talented young instrumentalists aged 5-17 who, because of financial need, may be prevented from fulfilling their creative potential. Grants of between £200 and £2,000 are available, based on evidence of musical talent and financial need. Award payments are made to institutions, music organisations, music teachers and other suppliers. Awards are not made directly to students or their families. All applications are means tested.

Awards are made to help with costs such as:

- Buying or hiring a musical instrument
- Music lessons
- Weekend music schools

- Music courses
- Orchestra fees
- Travel

Contact: Caroline Harvie, Awards for Young Musicians, PO Box 2754, Bristol, BS4 9DA

Tel: 0117 904 9906
Email: enquiries@a-y-m.org.uk
Website: www.a-y-m.org.uk

Youth Music Open Programme

The Open Programme is available for organisations wishing to apply for grants of £5,000 to £30,000.

Open Programme funded projects need to support one of the following goals:

- **Early Years** – advancing the learning and development of all children in their early years (0-5) by aiming to ensure universal access to high quality music making in England.
- **Challenging Circumstances** – improving life chances in the most challenging circumstances by supporting young people to achieve their full potential through engagement and progression in music making.
- **Encouraging Talent and Potential** – realising musical talent and potential by ensuring opportunity for all to develop their talent regardless of background or chosen genre.

Contact: Youth Music, Suites 3-5, Swan Court, 9 Tanner Street, London, SE1 3LE

Tel: 0207 902 1060
Email: info@youthmusic.org.uk
Website: www.youthmusic.org.uk

Arts Council Grants

Arts Council Grants champion, develop and invest in artistic experiences that enrich people's lives. Grants are for individuals, arts organisations and other people who use the arts in their work. They support activities that engage people, or that help artists and arts organisations in England to carry out their work.

Contact: Arts Council England, 14 Great Peter Street, London, SW1P 3NQ

Tel: 0845 3006200 or 0845 300 6100
Website: www.artscouncil.org.uk/funding

The BRIT Trust

The trust offers funding to encourage young people in the exploration and pursuit of educational, cultural or therapeutic benefits emanating from music. The BRIT Trust will only support projects within the UK. Applications are considered annually and must be received by August for projects planned for the following year.

Contact: The BRIT Trust, Riverside Building, County Hall, Westminster Bridge Road, London, SE1 7JA

Tel: 0207 803 1300
Email: brittrust@bpi.co.uk
Website: www.brittrust.co.uk

Sedgemoor District Council Grants Programme

Sedgemoor District Council offers three funding streams, designed to benefit the people of Sedgemoor:

- **Village Hall and Community Centre Capital Grant Scheme** – offers grants of up to £10,000 for projects that are of a capital nature that will improve the use of the building and enhance sustainability, for example by improving energy efficiency to reduce on-going running costs.
- **Community Health Fund** – up to £2,000 for projects, classes or activities that fit into the themes of increasing physical activity, weight management or increasing healthy eating.
- **Small Grants funding** – up to £1,000 for projects that fit into the broad themes of Community, Environment, Arts and Sports.

Contact: Rob Semple, Community Development Project Officer, Sedgemoor District Council, Bridgwater House, King Square, Bridgwater, TA6 3AR

Tel: 01278 436439
Email: community.services@sedgemoor.gov.uk
Website: www.sedgemoor.gov.uk

Community and Voluntary Sector Grants Taunton Deane

This fund has been created to support organisations and projects that seek to improve the lives, health and wellbeing of people in Taunton Deane, and to help organisations to become sustainable for the future.

Financial assistance is available for local groups and organisations to help with their running costs or delivery costs of projects that benefit the residents of Taunton Deane. Applications can be made for up to £5,000, but in most cases support grants will be much smaller. Only one grant will be awarded per organisation each year.

Contact: Strategy Team, Taunton Deane Borough Council, The Deane House, Belvedere Road, Taunton, Somerset, TA1 1HE

Tel: 01823 356312
Email: strategy@tauntondeane.gov.uk
Website: www.tauntondeane.gov.uk

South Somerset District Council Community Grants

SSDC is committed to supporting innovative communities that seek help to help themselves. The community grants programme can support voluntary and charitable organisations, not-for-profit groups, parish or town councils and other organisations that benefit the wider community. The main programme of community grants can fund up to 50 per cent of project costs to a maximum of £12,500.

Tel: 01458 257405 (North Area)   01963 435023 (East Area)
        01935 462787 (South Area)   01460 260423 (West Area)

Website: www.southsomerset.gov.uk/communities/funding-and-support-for-your-community

Funding Central

This website is funded by the Cabinet Office – Office for Civil Society and provides a guide to over 4,000 grants, contracts and loans. When you register with the site you can personalise your preferences to ensure you receive updates that are of interest to you.

Website: www.fundingcentral.org.uk

GRANTnet

This is a free-to-use online service, which can help small businesses, charitable and community groups find suitable funding as well as offering related guidance. The site contains information on over 5,000 funding opportunities that are available in the UK from European and national sources. Whilst the site is free, you do need to register in order to be able to use it.

Website: www.grantnet.com

Somerset Youth & Community Service
Tips on applying for funding

1. Does your project meet the criteria of the funding? If you are not sure, speak to someone at the funding organisation to check before submitting your application.

2. Check what the deadline for applications is and make sure you allow plenty of time. It is unlikely that funders will be able to extend the deadline if you have a last minute IT disaster, for example.

3. Read the application form and any guidance thoroughly.

4. If you're not sure of anything about the funding, speak to the funder for advice.

5. Check what, if any, supporting documents are required and make sure you enclose them. Ensure all documents have your group's name on them.

6. Don't send any additional supporting documents unless they are relevant.

7. Keep a photocopy of your application.

8. Work out your budget carefully and make sure all your figures are clear, add up properly and are realistic.

9. Do not automatically apply for the maximum amount; only apply for what you need.

10. Provide contact details where a member of your organisation can reliably be reached during office hours.

11. Make sure all necessary signatures are on the form before it is sent.

12. Ask someone who is not familiar with your project to read through the application to make sure it clearly explains the project to someone who has no knowledge of it. It should clearly communicate who you are and what you do.

13. Make sure your application looks good and is neat and legible.

14. Demonstrate that there is a need and/or demand for the project.

15. Show enthusiasm for your project, but be objective.

16. Make sure you have all the required policies and procedures in place.

17. Carefully proofread your application before submitting it.

18. Respond to any requests for additional information promptly.

Sample Health and Safety Statement

This is the Health and Safety Policy Statement of <Name of Organisation>

Our statement of general policy is to:

- Adhere to the health and safety policy of the premises (this should form the bulk of your policy).

- Adhere to the fire regulations of the premises.

- Provide adequate control of the health and safety risks arising out of our activities.

- Carry out risk assessments on activities inside and outside the club and revise as appropriately.

- Consult with our employees/volunteers (as appropriate) on matters affecting their health and safety.

- Provide and maintain safe plant and equipment.

- Ensure safe handling and use of substances.

- Provide information, instruction and supervision for employees/volunteers.

- Ensure all employees/volunteers are competent to do their tasks.

- Give all employees/volunteers adequate training.

- Prevent accidents and cases of work-related ill health.

- Maintain safe and healthy working conditions.

- Review and revise the policy and this statement as necessary at regular intervals.

Signed: ....
                 (Block capitals)

Position: ....

Date: ....Review date: ....

Internet Policy Sample

\<Name of Organisation\> has provided internet enabled computers for the use of the young people who attend the youth club. It is the policy of **\<Name of Organisation\>** that:

- Each computer is fitted with appropriate protection software to filter out sites that are unsuitable for young people. However, it must be remembered that this software is not infallible and young people must agree not to access inappropriate sites from youth club computers.

- Young people will be told by a member of staff what appropriate use of the internet is before using it (see below). Young people must agree to abide by the rules of usage before being allowed to use the equipment.

- A member of staff will be present when young people are using the internet. Staff will attempt to monitor internet use, but in practice **\<Name of Organisation\>** cannot guarantee close supervision of internet use.

- Parents will be informed about the availability of internet connections at the youth club on the annual parental consent form.

- Young people will be able to access social networking sites, as well as other internet sites, as this is an important part of their social life.

- Bullying will not be tolerated. Any young person found to have used the **\<Name of Organisation\>**'s IT equipment to bully other young people will be banned from using the IT equipment and possibly the youth club. The length of the ban will depend on the nature of the bullying. In severe cases, the young person may be banned from youth club permanently and parents informed.

- Accessing inappropriate internet sites will not be tolerated. Any young person found to have used the **\<Name of Organisation\>**'s IT equipment to access inappropriate sites will be banned from using the IT equipment and possibly the youth club. The length of the ban will depend on the nature of the inappropriate access. In severe cases, the young person may be banned from youth club permanently and parents informed.

  Appropriate use of the internet by young people includes:

  - Accessing only age appropriate sites;
  - Not accessing sites containing overtly sexual or violent content;
  - Not using the equipment to bully or harass other young people, either individually or in groups;
  - Not accessing sites that incite hatred of others.

Signed: Date:

On behalf of **\<Name of Organisation\>** Management Committee

Risk Assessment Policy Sample

<Name of Organisation> adheres to the 1992 Management of Safety Regulations, which require risk assessment to be carried out on all activities where hazards can arise out of the activity and other factors in the venue.

- A hazard is defined as something with the potential to cause harm.
- A risk expresses the likelihood that the harm from a particular hazard is realised.
- The extent of the risk covers the number of people who might be exposed to the risk and the consequences for them.

The management committee of **<Name of Organisation>** will ensure that all activities are risk assessed and the results recorded in writing. These assessments, together with the required control measures, will be shared with all staff involved in the activity.

All risk assessments will be reviewed, either when there is a change in the nature of the activity or annually (whichever is sooner).

<Name of Organisation> uses the Health and Safety Executive's *Five Steps to Risk Assessment* as its method for assessing and managing risk. These steps are:

Five Steps to Risk Assessment

Step 1 – Look for hazards.

Step 2 - Decide who might be harmed and how.

Step 3 – Evaluate the risks and decide whether the existing precautions are adequate or whether more should be done.

Step 4 – Record your findings.

Step 5 – Review your assessment and revise it if necessary, but at least annually.

All current risk assessments will be kept on site and be available to all staff.

Signed: _____   Print name: _____

Date: _____

Review date: _____

{N.B. This document can be combined with the Health and Safety Policy.}

© Somerset Youth and Community Service 2013

<Name of Organisation> recognises the growing concern among health experts about the risks to the health of those who smoke and those do not smoke but are exposed to tobacco smoke.

<Name of Organisation> acknowledges that young people should be discouraged from smoking.

Smoking in <Name of Organisation> premises and vehicles:
- In addition to the current smoking ban in all public places, smoking will not be permitted at any time on **<Name of Organisation>** premises. A designated smoking area has been identified at **<Name/Description of Location>** and suitable bins have been provided. Staff (paid or unpaid) should seek to ensure that young people and visitors smoke only in designated areas.

- All **<Name of Organisation>** vehicles will be smoke-free. Where our vehicles are used to provide a transport service, users must not smoke in the vehicle.

Staff and smoking at work/during youth club sessions and activities:
- Staff (paid or unpaid) must not smoke in front of young people whilst working.

- Staff (paid or unpaid) must not give to young people, or buy for young people cigarettes or tobacco or any associated paraphernalia (this includes lights, papers and filters).

- Staff (paid or unpaid) must not receive from young people cigarettes or tobacco or any associated paraphernalia (this includes lights, papers and filters).

- Staff (paid or unpaid) taking part in trips or residentials with young people are expected to take reasonable steps to smoke only during designated breaks and out of the company of young people.

- As evening sessions are **<X>** hours in length, staff (paid or unpaid) are not expected to take smoking breaks during sessions.

- Where staff (paid or unpaid) enter into private households as part of their work, they must refrain from smoking.

- Staff (paid or unpaid) who fail to observe the requirements of this smoking policy make themselves liable to action under the disciplinary and appeals procedure, which could ultimately lead to dismissal.

<Name of Organisation> Smoking Policy will be included in recruitment literature and all prospective employees/volunteers should be informed that **<Name of Organisation>** provides a smoke-free work environment.

The effectiveness of this policy will be regularly reviewed.

Signed: Date:

On behalf of **<Name of Organisation>** Management Committee.

Sample Staff Employment and Management Policy

Introduction

This policy covers the following topics:

1. Recruitment, appointment and probation
2. Hours of work and holidays
3. Management and supervision
4. Payment
5. Training
6. Sickness absence
7. Maternity/paternity/adoption leave
8. Termination of employment
9. Disciplinary procedure
10. Grievance procedure
11. Equality and diversity
12. Bullying and harassment
13. Data protection/Action against fraud

This policy applies to all staff, whether paid or unpaid.

1. Recruitment, appointment and probation

All posts will be advertised locally and candidates will be provided with a copy of the job description and person specification for the post advertised, along with information about the youth club. Interviews, based on the person specification, will be held. Records of the outcomes of these interviews will be kept confidentially. Candidates will be told within two weeks of their interview, in writing, if they are to be offered a post.

The offer of a post is reliant on the satisfactory completion of an Enhanced DBS check. Any offer will be withdrawn if the check reveals that the candidate is unsuitable to work with young people.

On acceptance of a post, the prospective staff member will be sent a letter of confirmation and written statement of employment.

Confirmation of employment will be subject to the satisfactory completion of a probationary period of **<three/six>** months. During probationary service, the staff member will be expected to establish their suitability for the job. Staff will be informed in writing as to whether or not they have successfully completed their probationary period. Failure to complete successfully may lead to dismissal.

2. Hours of work and holidays

Staff hours of work are detailed in their written statement of employment and offer letter. Staff will occasionally be required to work weekends or evenings, by negotiation.

Overtime will not be paid. Additional hours and time off in lieu must be agreed in advance with the line manager.

Staff are entitled to 25 days holiday (pro rata) per year. This excludes public holidays, for which staff will receive pro rata paid time off. The holiday year begins on 1st April. Unused entitlement may not be carried forward to the next holiday year. Leave is taken by negotiation and approval from the line manager.

3. Management and supervision

All staff, paid or unpaid, will receive an hour-long line management meeting once every two months. Notes will be taken by the manager at supervision meetings and kept confidentially. Copies will be given to the member of staff.

The chairperson of the management committee will manage the staff member in charge of the youth club. Other staff (paid and unpaid) will be line managed by the staff member in charge of the youth club.

Staff meetings will be held termly for two hours. Attendance is obligatory.

4. Payment

Where staff are paid, rates of pay will be stated on the job description. Pay and price increases will be considered by the management committee annually, in April of each year. Annual pay and price increases are not guaranteed.

Staff annual salary will be divided into twelve monthly payments, to be made via bank transfer on the 1st of each month. Payment is made in arrears.

5. Training

The management committee is committed to encouraging and offering training to all its staff (paid or unpaid).

All staff will have an induction to the organisation and the committee will ensure that training opportunities are offered to all staff, including first aid, child protection, risk assessment and health and safety awareness. Paid staff have two days' training time included in their contracts. Where appropriate and resources allow, the committee will pay for relevant courses and staff will be reimbursed for any travelling expenses incurred.

All staff will be given access to copies of the organisation's policies.

6. Sickness absence

Staff are entitled to contractual sick pay at their normal rate of pay for a maximum of **<number of weeks>** *{recommended 1 week}* (pro rata) for any one period of incapacity. Staff are entitled to a maximum of **<number of weeks>** *{recommended 4 weeks}* sick pay (pro rata) in any one year.

This is subject to the requirements to notify the employer and provide evidence of incapacity. Thereafter, staff may be entitled to statutory sick pay.

Sickness absence must be reported to the line manager as early as possible on the first day of sickness and each subsequent day when staff are unable to work. Failure to notify will result in the loss of contractual sick pay.

Self-certification is allowed for a maximum of 5 days, after which a doctor's certificate must be provided.

7. Maternity/paternity/adoption leave

Under the provision of the Employment Rights Act 1996 (as amended by the Employment Act 2002 and associated regulations) staff are entitled to maternity/paternity/adoption leave.

8. Termination of employment

This employment is permanent subject to each party's right to terminate in accordance with the terms of this statement. Both staff and employer must give [number of weeks] *{recommended 1 month}* notice to terminate employment.

9. Disciplinary procedure

The following procedure will be followed when an employee is being disciplined or dismissed. The procedure provides that in normal cases an employee will be given a series of warnings before disciplinary penalty or dismissal is contemplated. The stages of the procedure apply when a disciplinary penalty, e.g. demotion or dismissal, is applied.

Matters which may be dealt with under this disciplinary and dismissal procedure include discipline and dismissal related to:

- misconduct;
- sub-standard performance;
- harassment or victimisation of colleagues, young people or community members;
- misuse of the organisation's facilities including computer facilities (e.g. email and the internet);
- poor timekeeping;
- unauthorised absences.

Minor cases of misconduct and most cases of poor performance can often be dealt with by informal advice, coaching and counselling. An informal verbal warning may be given, which does not count as part of the formal disciplinary procedure. No formal record of this type of warning will be kept. If there is no improvement or the matter is serious enough, staff will be invited to a disciplinary meeting at which the matter can be properly discussed. Staff are allowed to bring a work colleague or trade union representative to the meeting. The outcome of the meeting will be communicated to staff. There are the following possible outcomes:

Verbal warning
In the case of minor infringements, staff may be given a formal verbal warning. A note of the verbal warning will be kept on staff files but will be disregarded for disciplinary purposes after a specified period {e.g. six months}. The staff member concerned has the right to appeal against a formal verbal warning.

Written warning
If the infringement is more serious or there is no improvement in conduct after a formal verbal warning, staff will be given a formal written warning giving details of the complaint, the improvement or change in behaviour required, the timescale allowed for this, the right of appeal and the fact that a final written warning may be given if there is no sustained satisfactory improvement or change. A copy of the written warning will be kept on file but will be disregarded for disciplinary purposes after a specified period {e.g. 12 months}.

Final written warning
Where there is a failure to improve or change behaviour while a formal written warning is still in effect, or where the infringement is sufficiently serious, staff may be given a final written warning. This will give details of the complaint, warn that failure to improve will lead to dismissal and refer to the right of appeal. The final written warning will be kept on file but will normally be disregarded for disciplinary purposes after a specified period {e.g. 18 months}.

Dismissal
If a staff member's conduct or performance still fails to improve, the final stage will be to contemplate dismissal, or to take action short of dismissal, e.g. demotion. If the application of a disciplinary penalty or dismissal is contemplated, the management committee will begin the following procedure:

Step 1: Staff are given a written statement and called to a meeting to discuss the matter.
The committee will set out in writing the staff member's alleged conduct, characteristics or other circumstances which led the committee to contemplate dismissing or taking disciplinary action against the staff member. The committee will also set out the basis on which it has made the allegations. If possible, the committee will provide the staff member with copies of relevant evidence. The committee will invite the member of staff to a hearing to discuss the matter.

Step 2: Meeting is held and employer informs employee of the outcome.
The meeting will take place before any disciplinary action, other than suspension on full pay, is taken. The meeting will be held without undue delay but only when the member of staff has had a reasonable opportunity to consider their response to the written statement and any further verbal explanation given. The member of staff must take all reasonable steps to attend the meeting.

After the meeting the committee will inform the staff member of its decision and notify the member of staff of their right to appeal if they are not satisfied.

Step 3: Appeal against the disciplinary decision if necessary.
If a staff member wishes to appeal, they must inform the management committee chairperson in writing within a reasonable time *{recommended 10 working days}*.

If this is done, the committee will invite the member of staff to attend a further meeting. The member of staff must take all reasonable steps to attend the meeting. If practicable, a more senior manager not previously involved in the disciplinary procedure will hear the appeal.

The appeal hearing may take place before or after dismissal or disciplinary action has taken effect. After the appeal hearing the committee will inform the employee of its final decision and confirm it in writing as soon as practicable *{recommended 5 days}*.

Gross misconduct
If, after investigation, it is confirmed that an employee has committed one of the following offences (the list is not exhaustive), they will normally be dismissed without notice or payment in lieu of notice:

- theft;
- fraud or deliberate falsification of records;
- physical violence;
- serious bullying or harassment of colleagues, young people or community members;
- deliberate damage to property;
- serious insubordination;
- misuse of the organisation's property or name;
- bringing the employer into serious disrepute;
- serious incapability whilst on duty brought on by alcohol or illegal drugs;
- serious negligence, which causes or might cause unacceptable loss, damage or injury;
- serious infringement of health and safety rules;
- serious breach of confidence (subject to the Public Interest (Disclosure) Act 1998);
- inappropriate behaviour with young people.

While the alleged gross misconduct is being investigated, staff may be suspended, during which time they will be paid. In most cases any decision to dismiss will be taken only after a full investigation into the matter.

However, in a few cases of gross misconduct, the committee may be justified in dismissing immediately, without conducting an investigation. In these cases a two-step procedure will be followed:

Step 1: The committee give the employee a written statement.
The committee will provide a written statement setting out the conduct that resulted in immediate dismissal and informing the staff member of the right to appeal against the decision to dismiss.

Step 2: Appeal against the decision to dismiss.
If the employee wishes to appeal, they must inform the chairperson of management committee. A meeting must be held (in accordance with the general principles set out above). The committee will then inform the employee of the decision as soon as possible after the meeting.

General principles applicable to the procedures.
The following principles apply to the dismissal procedure set out above:

1. The person who has authority to discipline in accordance with this procedure is the staff member's line manager.
2. Staff have the right to be accompanied to any meeting by a trade union representative or co-worker.
3. Each step in the procedure will be taken without unreasonable delay and hearings will be held at reasonable times and locations.
4. Meetings will be conducted in a manner that enables both the staff member and the committee to explain their cases.
5. The committee will keep records detailing the nature of any breach of disciplinary rules or unsatisfactory performance, staff defence or mitigation, the action taken and the reasons for it, whether an appeal was lodged, its outcome and any subsequent developments. The committee will keep these records confidential.

10. Grievance procedure

It is committee policy to ensure that any employee with a grievance has access to a procedure that can lead to a fair and speedy resolution of the matter.

Most routine complaints and grievances are best resolved informally in discussion with the immediate line manager. Where the grievance cannot be resolved informally it will be dealt with under the following procedure:

The standard grievance procedure.

Step 1: Staff member gives the committee a written statement of their grievance.
The staff member must put their grievance in a written statement and send a copy to the chairperson of the management committee. Where the grievance is against this individual, the matter should be raised with a more senior manager if there is one.

Step 2: A meeting is held and the committee informs the staff member of the outcome.
The committee will invite the member of staff to a meeting to discuss the grievance. The meeting will only take place once the staff member has

informed the committee of the basis for the grievance they have set out in their written statement, and the committee has had a reasonable opportunity to consider what response to make. The staff member must take all reasonable steps to attend the meeting.

As soon as possible after the meeting, the committee will inform the member of staff of the decision taken in response to the grievance and notify them of their right to appeal if they are not satisfied with it.

Step 3: Appeal if necessary.

If the member of staff then wishes to appeal they must inform the committee within 10 days and it will invite them to an appeal hearing. The staff member must take all reasonable steps to attend. If reasonably practicable, a more senior manager who has not been involved in the grievance procedure so far will deal with the appeal. As soon as possible after the hearing, the committee will inform the staff member of their decision, which will be final.

Raising grievances after you have left the organisation.

If staff wish to raise a grievance after they have left the organisation's employment, they must follow a two-step procedure:

Step 1: The staff member gives the committee a written statement of their grievance.

The staff member must put their grievance in a written statement and send a copy to the chairperson of the management committee.

Step 2: The committee will give the member of staff a written response.

The committee will write back to the staff member giving their response to the points raised.

General principles applicable to the procedures.

1. The committee will carry out each step in the procedure without unreasonable delay and arrange meetings at reasonable times and locations.
2. Meetings will be conducted in a way that allows both parties to explain their case.
3. Records will be kept detailing the nature of the grievance raised, the response, any action taken and the reasons for it. These records will be kept confidential.
4. Staff have the right to be accompanied to the hearing by a trade union representative or a colleague.

11. Equality and diversity

The committee is committed to creating a culture that promotes equality for children, young people and the staff that work with them. We recognise that discrimination is harmful to well-being.

The committee promotes equality by creating a culture within the organisation where equality is at the core of all activities and the committee works toward the elimination of discrimination, both direct and indirect, and any form of bullying. The committee strives to ensure fairness, impartiality and consistency in all working practices. The committee ensures all staff and volunteers are carefully selected and that they accept responsibility for helping to prevent discrimination within the organisation.

12. Bullying and harassment

The committee will not tolerate any form of bullying or harassment. Bullying and harassment includes verbal abuse, violence, insulting or offensive behaviour, or behaviour that humiliates others (this is not an exhaustive list).

Members of staff found to be carrying out any of these behaviours during work-related activities (including social events) may be disciplined and could ultimately be dismissed (see the disciplinary procedure above).

Staff should discuss any complaints with their line manager. If this is not appropriate, any other officer of the committee can be spoken to. The grievance and disciplinary procedures detailed above will be used to deal with any incidents in the workplace.

Any complaint will be taken seriously, treated confidentially and staff making a complaint will be protected from retaliation.

A thorough investigation will take place and there will be a right to appeal.

13. Data protection/Action against fraud

Staff have a duty to ensure that they comply with the requirements of the Data Protection Act 1984 and its associated guidance.

If staff are data users under the terms of the act, they should ensure that personal data is obtained, held, processed and disclosed legally.

Should staff require further information concerning this legislation they should contact their line manager.

Payroll information held about staff may be used to prevent and detect fraud. The <Name of Organisation> management committee may also share this information, for the same purposes, with other organisations that handle public funds. Any data generated will be destroyed when enquiries are complete.

Signed: _____ Date: _____

Chair of <Name of Organisation> Management Committee

Printed Name: _____

Review Date: _____

Staff Vetting Policy

1. All regular staff (paid or voluntary) of **<Name of Organisation>** are required to hold a Criminal Records Certificate prior to working unsupervised with young people. DBS checks will be repeated every 3 years.

2. All members of the management committee, who have access to young people or their records, are required to undergo an Enhanced Disclosure and Barring Service check. The DBS checks will be repeated every 3 years.

3. Occasional parent helpers will not be required to have a DBS check as they will always be supervised by regular staff.

4. It is the responsibility of the management committee to ensure that every regular staff member has a valid DBS certificate. Until a representative of the management committee sees the certificate the staff member will not have unsupervised responsibility for any young people.

5. A management committee representative will provide the forms and pay the cost for the staff members to have their DBS checks carried out. This will be done via **<Insert name of preferred umbrella organisation>**.

6. All volunteers who seek to work with young people should complete an application form before any involvement with young people is considered.

   a. A transient lifestyle, indicated by frequent changes of address and changes of name (other than change on marriage), will be investigated. Adults who have harmed young people tend to move around and use aliases.

   b. Criminal convictions range from the minor (e.g. parking offences) to the very serious (e.g. rape and murder) and for the purposes of applying to work with young people, convictions are never spent.

7. The staff (paid or unpaid) application form will ask for:

   a. Personal details (name, addresses for the past three years, date of birth, National Insurance number and current occupation);

   b. Competencies and areas of interest;

   c. The names of two independent referees;

   d. Any criminal convictions.

Signed: ………………………….. ………………………………….
(Block capitals)

Date: …………………………….

Review date: …………………………….

{N.B. This could be combined with the Child Protection Policy into a Safeguarding Policy.}

© Somerset Youth and Community Service 2013

Training Policy Sample

<Name of Organisation> management committee is committed to encouraging and offering training to all its staff whether paid or unpaid.

All staff will have an induction to **<Name of Organisation>** and the committee will endeavour to ensure that training opportunities are offered to voluntary staff, including:

- First aid
- Child protection
- Risk assessment and health & safety awareness

<Name of Organisation> management committee is committed to training in line with the child protection policy to ensure a safe environment is provided for all young people attending its youth club.

All staff will be given access to copies of **<Name of Organisation>**'s policies.

Where appropriate, **<Name of Organisation>** will pay for relevant courses and staff will be reimbursed for any travelling expenses incurred.

Signed: Date:

Block Capitals:

Position:

On behalf of **<Name of Organisation>** Management Committee.

Accident and Incident Report Sample

This report should be completed immediately after any accident or incident has occurred. One copy should be retained by the leader of the group and a copy given to **<Insert name of Management Committee member responsible>**. Insert one copy into the Accident and Incident folder and discuss what follow up action is necessary.

Name of Group:

Day, date and time of incident:

What are the names, addresses and ages of those involved in the incident?

Where did this incident take place?

Who is normally responsible for the group? (Name, address and telephone number.)

Who was responsible for the group at the time of the incident, if different from the above? (Name, address and telephone number.)

Which other workers were supervising the group at the time of the incident? (Names, addresses and telephone numbers.)

Who witnessed the incident? (Names, addresses, telephone numbers and ages if under 16. Normally two witnesses will be needed.)

Describe the accident/incident (include injuries and any first aid or medical treatment given).

Have you retained any defective equipment? (Yes/No/None involved)

Yes		No		None Involved	

If so where is it being kept and by whom?

What actions have you taken to prevent a re-occurrence of the incident?

Is the site or premises still safe for your group to use?

	Yes		No	

Is the equipment still safe for your group to use?

	Yes		No	

Who else do you need to inform?

Have they been informed?

	Yes		No	

Signature of person in charge of the group at the time of the accident/incident:

Signature:		Date:	

Appendix 17

Activity Risk Assessment Sample

Risk Assessment of: **Kittenford Youth Centre**   Assessor: **Hengist Brown**   Date: **January 2013**

Overview of activity: Playing pool

Is assessment generic or (specific)?

(*circle as appropriate)

Context of assessment: planning stage*/'desk top' exercise*/(site visit*)/consultation with managers*/other* (please describe):

(*circle as appropriate)

Hazard(s) identified	Persons affected	Existing controls	Additional controls required
Balls flying off pool table and hitting someone. Accidental damage to table. Someone accidentally injured with cue.	Staff and young people	• Table is a safe distance from seating area. • Table in full view of staff. • Only players allowed around table. • No food or drink allowed near or on table. • Young people understand how to play pool.	
Balls being thrown. Chalk being thrown. Cues being used as weapons.	Staff and young people	• Balls, cues and chalk put away when not in use and kept securely. • Ground rules understood by young people. • Table in full view of staff.	

Signed: _____   Date: _____

Annual Consent Form Sample

<Club Name> **<Address>** **<Phone number>**	**<Club Logo>**

Annual Parental Consent Form

For Young People aged under 18: **<September 20XX to August 20XX>**

Dear Parent or Carer

Your daughter/son has expressed a wish to take part in activities at **<Name of Organisation>**. Please sign and return this form as soon as possible to the address above, or to the club. **If the forms are not returned your daughter or son may be unable to come to the <XXXX> Youth Club.**

Many different activities form part of our club programme. These activities include barbeques, picnics, sports and games (both indoor and outdoor), interclub visits, competitions, arts, crafts, town/village treasure hunts, attendance at **<Name of Organisation>** management meetings, quizzes, discussions and cooking. If there are any you would prefer your daughter or son not to take part in, then you should list them in the box provided below. We will assume that activities not listed in the box have received your consent.

I do **not** wish my daughter or son to participate in the following activities: PLEASE LEAVE BLANK IF YOU HAVE NO OBJECTIONS

We will ask for additional consent for any activities that take place outside the main vicinity of the youth club and require organised travel. We will also ask for additional consent for your daughter/son to take part in adventurous, hazardous or residential activities.

Conduct: In order for all young people to have an enjoyable time there have to be certain ground rules that must be followed at all times. These include participants refraining from any behaviour that places a young person, member of staff or member of the public at risk (for example bullying, vandalism, the misuse of drugs or alcohol). We ask for your support in ensuring these rules are adhered to. Although young people are encouraged to remain on the premises during a youth work session we are not able to force them to do so.

Photography: We may take individual or group photographs of young people taking part in activities that may then be used for displays, in publications we produce or on selected websites. We may also make video or webcam recordings of activities and take photographs or film footage in which young people may appear, sometimes named, in local or national newspapers or on television. If you have any objections please state them in writing in the box below.

Please state any objection:
PLEASE LEAVE BLANK IF YOU HAVE NO OBJECTION

Internet and email: We may make computer systems available to young people so they can access email and the internet. Any objections to the use of this equipment should be noted in the box below. If you want more information about our policies around young people's use of computer equipment, please contact **<Name of Organisation>**.

Please state any objection:
PLEASE LEAVE BLANK IF YOU HAVE NO OBJECTION

Additional information: If there are any other issues which you believe staff should be aware of (e.g. related to faith or religion) please note them below:

Medical Information: Please give us any medical information that you think may be relevant (for example, medical conditions, current medications or allergies).
I agree to my son/daughter receiving medical care if required. This would include first aid and any emergency dental, medical or surgical treatment as considered necessary by the medical authorities present in the best interest of your son/daughter. Please tick here if you **do not** agree ☐

I have read, fully understood and am satisfied with the details supplied about the above-mentioned activities and agree to my daughter or son taking part in them. I know of no medical reason why they should not participate and I am happy with arrangements outlined above regarding photography and behaviour.

Young person's name:	Date of birth:
Parent or carer's name:	Parent or carer's signature:

Emergency Contact Details

Name of Parent/Guardian:	
Address:	
Emergency telephone:	Daytime: Evening: Mobile:

Alternative emergency contact should parents/guardians not be available:

Name:		Relationship to child	
Address:			
Telephone	Daytime: Evening: Mobile		

Appendix 19

Bowling and McDonald's Trip Risk Assessment

Sample

<Name of Organisation> Bowling and McDonald's Trip Risk Assessment	Written by:	Date:	Next review date:

What's the hazard?	What is already being done to control the risks?	What further action is recommended to reduce risks?	Action by whom?	Date action due	Date action done
Car accidents, trips, slips and losing young people between car park and Bowlplex/McDonald's	• Park as close to Bowlplex/McDonald's in car park as possible, ensuring side access doors do not open into the road. • Brief young people about being aware of potential hazards created by other vehicles in the area. • Staff to supervise young people around the car park area. • Group is to stay together and use footpath where possible to access Bowlplex/McDonald's. • Group to avoid walking in the road, where possible, and to be patient if cars are moving in or out of parking spaces.				

What's the hazard?	What is already being done to control the risks?	What further action is recommended to reduce risks?	Action by whom?	Date action due	Date action done
Stranger danger	• Young people warned of stranger danger. • Young people agree to not talk to strangers and let staff know immediately if they have any concerns. • Young people advised to go to the toilets in pairs.				
Bowling – sprains, bruising, crush injuries	• Young people to be made aware of the potential harm heavy bowling balls can cause. • Ensure young people either wear or bring socks to wear during the activity. • Bowling balls to remain on the rack when not in use. • Only one person on the bowling alley at a time. • When not bowling, rest of the group to remain at seating area until their turn. • Young people advised on safe technique for bowling.				

What's the hazard?	What is already being done to control the risks?	What further action is recommended to reduce risks?	Action by whom?	Date action due	Date action done
Behaviour – anti-social behaviour, young people getting lost	<ul><li>Staff to supervise young people and monitor their behaviour.</li><li>Brief young people before the activity about acceptable behaviour within a public environment and young people agree ground rules.</li><li>Parents have signed consent forms for the trip, which state acceptable behaviour.</li><li>Staff have positive relationship with young people.</li><li>Ensure young people have the contact number for member of staff on the trip in case they get lost from the group.</li><li>Brief young people about where to meet after the activity has finished so that no one gets lost.</li><li>Ensure staff have mobile numbers for young people on the trip in case they get separated after the activity and in order to be able to locate them.</li><li>Young people agree to stay with the group.</li></ul>				

What's the hazard?	What is already being done to control the risks?	What further action is recommended to reduce risks?	Action by whom?	Date action due	Date action done
McDonald's	• Ensure adequate staff supervision of young people walking between minibus and cars and restaurant and within restaurant. • Ensure staff have mobile contact numbers for young people on trip and vice versa. • Ensure young people are aware of departure time. • Ensure staff aware of any food allergies identified on consent forms. • Staff will supervise young people at all times in McDonald's.				
Emergency – accident, incident, illness	• Young people and their parents/carers informed of contact numbers of staff on trip. • Staff have a record of emergency contact numbers for parents/carers of all young people. • Staff are first aid trained and have first aid kit with them. • Staff have access to a phone if an ambulance or a parent's presence is needed.				

Please now pass this assessment to the Chair of the Management Committee for approval

Name of Chair		Date:		Signature:

Building Risk Assessment Sample

<Name of Organisation> Building Risk Assessment	Written by:	Date:	Next review date:

What is the hazard?	What is already being done to control the risk?	What further action is recommended?	Action by whom?	Date action due	Date action done
Water – leak, damage to property and injury to self	• Key holders and hirers are aware of stopcock location. • Ensure that warning notices are in place when buckets are on floor to catch drips from leaking roof.				
Movement – through corridors, blocking fire exits, trip hazards	• All areas to be kept clear of obstructions. • Joins in floor covering to be maintained in good condition. • Check area before each session. • Ensure steps outside office are kept clear of obstructions. • Storage space provided to stop equipment being stored in corridors or being left out.	Monitor communications book	Admin	Ongoing	

What is the hazard?	What is already being done to control the risk?	What further action is recommended?	Action by whom?	Date action due	Date action done
Storage – sprains and falling equipment	• Ensure equipment is stored tidily in cupboards so that it will stay in place when cupboard door is opened. • Bulky and heavy items not to be stored above waist height.				
Maintaining a safe environment	• Fire extinguishers to be properly maintained. • No smoking anywhere in the building. • Certified first aider to be available at all times when young people use building. • All emergency signs to be maintained according to relevant standard. • Ensure health and safety checklist is kept up to date.				
Access to toilet facilities – buckets brooms, flipchart stored in accessible toilet	• Toilet storage kept to a minimum	Ensure user groups are aware of the need to put equipment away at end of sessions	Admin	October 2012	

What is the hazard?	What is already being done to control the risk?	What further action is recommended?	Action by whom?	Date action due	Date action done
Temperature of long radiator – very hot to touch, scalding. All users, particularly children as radiator at their height.	• Has been checked and OK	Need to monitor			
Gas – faulty equipment; affects all users if breakdown	• Visual inspection routine maintained. • Regular professional maintenance by qualified person.	Service history of appliances, need to be accessible and checked	Admin		
Use of electrical equipment – electrocution, fire, injury through faulty equipment (inc. fan systems etc.)	• Maintain equipment in good order. • Ensure PAT test and visual inspection routine maintained. • No flammable material to be stored close to computers or other electrical equipment. • No electrical equipment to be stored next to a water supply. • Users groups know location of shut off points.				

What is the hazard?	What is already being done to control the risk?	What further action is recommended?	Action by whom?	Date action due	Date action done
Manual Handling – chairs in hall, shelves in cupboard, pool table. Staff carrying material to and from venue. Moving furniture. Users groups attempting to lift heavy items of equipment/furniture – back injury, dropped items, fall.	• Pool table trolley to be used. • Ensure that loads are evenly distributed throughout vehicles. • Users groups discouraged from moving heavy items. • Although shelving in games room cupboard is a little insecure and not stable – things are now stored appropriately to minimize any risk. • Store items near to where they are used whenever possible.	Pool table trolley needed	Chair of Man. Com.	October 2012	
Use of step ladder – injury caused by falling, dropping items, back injury	• Bulky and heavy equipment not stored above shoulder height. • Step ladder inspected on regular basis. • Wherever possible step ladders not used by a lone worker.				
Use of cleaning equipment – chemical accidents	• All equipment to be kept in locked cupboards. • Cleaning materials only to be used by competent staff. • COSSH assessments are kept in cupboard and so accessible to all user groups. • Ensure protective equipment (e.g. gloves) is readily available.				

What is the hazard?	What is already being done to control the risk?	What further action is recommended?	Action by whom?	Date action due	Date action done
Noise – from karaoke, stereo, general talking and playing etc.	• User groups to monitor the volume of the stereo and karaoke and reduce it when necessary. • Ensure that users know what is acceptable and are encouraged to keep within that limit.				
Damage to building not being repaired – unsafe working practices for staff and other users	• Numbers for management committee available for user groups.				
Damage to property/equipment – financial risk, risk of injury through using damaged equipment or equipment malfunctioning	• User groups informed of appropriate and safe use of equipment, consequences of wilful damage and are encouraged to report to management committee if they notice anything is broken. • Accident/incident procedure and recording in place. • User groups to check safety of equipment before each session and repair/dispose of any damaged equipment.				
Power failure	• Ensure user groups know they need a plan concerning what to do if a power failure occurs, including the safe evacuation of users.				

© Somerset Youth and Community Service 2013

What is the hazard?	What is already being done to control the risk?	What further action is recommended?	Action by whom?	Date action due	Date action done
Use of kitchen – burns, cuts, hygiene	User groups advised that safe use of the kitchen includes: • Kitchen door to be left open at all times unless cooking is taking place with a responsible adult. • The serving hatch should be left open at all times. • Microwave and cooker only to be used under supervision of responsible adult. • Children or young people only to use kettle while supervised, or staff confident it is safe for them to do so. • When microwave, cooker or kettle in use, maximum of 2 young people allowed in kitchen with staff. • Sharp knives to be stored safely in drawer in kitchen. • Sharp knives not to be removed from the kitchen area. • All food preparation to be supervised by staff with a food hygiene qualification. • Cleaning and hygiene standards to be maintained by each user group.				

What is the hazard?	What is already being done to control the risk?	What further action is recommended?	Action by whom?	Date action due	Date action done
Road outside the building	<ul><li>Discourage young people from using road as extension of youth club.</li><li>Ensure young people are made aware of the dangers from cars.</li></ul>				
Cleanliness	<ul><li>Staff to regularly check cleanliness of building and action if necessary.</li><li>Staff to clean up at the end of each session.</li><li>Cleaning routine and hygiene standards to be maintained.</li></ul>				

What is the hazard?	What is already being done to control the risk?	What further action is recommended?	Action by whom?	Date action due	Date action done
Fire	• All user groups have regular fire drills. • No smoking anywhere in the building. • All emergency exit signs to be maintained according to relevant standard. • Ensure register taken every session. • Test fire alarm systems regularly. • Visual checks of fire extinguishers before each session. • Ensure fire exits are kept free of obstructions. • Ensure outside floor by fire exits is kept free from obstructions and algae.				
Arson	• Rubbish securely stored away from ignition sources and regularly collected. • Sources of ignition (cooker, lighters, matches etc.) supervised and not left outside.				

Please now pass this assessment to the Chair of the Management Committee for approval

Name of Chair	Date:	Chair's comments
Signature:		

Appendix 21

Coach Travel Risk Assessment Sample

<Name of Organisation> Coach Travel Risk Assessment	Written by: <Name of Writer>	Date:		Next review date:	

What is the hazard?	What will be done to control the risk?	What further action is recommended?	By whom?	Date action due	Date action done
Breakdown	• Hire coach from reputable company with breakdown cover. • Staff have parental contact details if needed (lateness, change of plan, cancellation). • If breakdown occurs, if possible move minibus over to side of road and supervise young people on verge ensuring they are a safe distance from the side of the road.				
Accident	• Ensure all passengers and driver wear seatbelts. • Stick to main roads for journey as far as possible. • Ensure no bags are stored in the aisle so that the aisle is kept clear. • Coach has fire extinguisher and first aid box. • Staff have parent contact numbers in case of accident. • Staff have medical information and medical consent if treatment is needed. • Staff have charged mobile phone(s).				

| Getting lost | • Route planned with coach company before trip.
• Stick to main roads where possible.
• Coach has SatNav or maps or staff have relevant knowledge. | | | | |

What is the hazard?	What will be done to control the risk?	What further action is recommended?	By whom?	Date action due	Date action done
Distracting the driver	• Staff supervise young people in the rear of the coach. • Behaviour ground rules agreed by young people before start of journey.				
Travel Sickness	• Information about whether or not young people get travel sick asked before the journey. • Sick bags and cleaning materials on the coach.				
Driver fatigue	• Breaks planned in journey where necessary. • Driver knows it's OK to take a break if needed.				

| Breaks in the journey – young people getting lost or behaving badly | <ul><li>Journey breaks kept to a minimum.</li><li>Young people have staff mobile phone numbers.</li><li>Staff have young people's mobile phone numbers.</li><li>Young people know where they are allowed and not allowed to go.</li><li>Young people know when to be back at the bus.</li><li>Behaviour ground rules agreed by young people before the trip.</li><li>Young people agree not to talk to strangers and are aware of 'stranger danger' and to inform staff of any concerns immediately.</li></ul> | | |

Please now pass this assessment to the Chair of the Management Committee for approval

Name of Chair	Date:	Signature:

Fire Prevention and Procedures Sample

FIRE EVACUATION PROCEDURE

Evacuation point – <Insert evacuation point here>

1. In the event of a fire one member of staff (nominated for the evening) should pick up the signing-in sheet and evacuate the young people from the **<Name of Venue>** and assemble them at **<Evacuation Point>**. Young people should not stop to collect personal belongings.
2. The other staff should check the toilets, cupboards and kitchen (**<Add other areas as necessary>**) to ensure that all young people have been cleared from the **<Name of Venue>**, closing doors behind them.
3. Staff will not tackle the fire with fire extinguishers unless they feel it is safe to do so.
4. The staff member in charge will then check the young people off the register.
5. The staff member in charge will call the Fire Service by dialling 999. No-one will re-enter the building until the Fire Service says it is safe to do so.

FIRE PREVENTION AND DRILL

1. Electrical appliances will be annually checked. However, any electrical item found to be faulty should not be used and should be reported to the staff member in charge.
2. Heaters and radiators will not be covered.
3. Flammable materials will not be stored close to heat sources and rubbish will be secured if stored outside the building.
4. A fire drill will be carried out at least once every four months to familiarise the young people with the procedure. Fire drills will be recorded.
5. The Emergency Evacuation Sheet will be displayed in the refreshment area.
6. Smoke detectors and emergency lighting are fitted in the **<Name of Venue>** and will be tested yearly.
7. Fire extinguishers will be checked and maintained yearly.
8. The register will include the names of the staff and any older young people who are helping.

Signed: Date:

On behalf of **<Name of Organisation>** Management Committee

{N.B. This can be combined with the Heath and Safety Policy/Statement.}

First Aid & Fire Sign

FIRST AID

FOR ALL FIRST AID EMERGENCIES

CONTACT YOUR NEAREST FIRST AIDER

WHO WILL HAVE ACCESS TO A FIRST AID BOX WHICH IS IN <LOCATIONS>

CHECK WHO THE FIRST AIDER FOR YOUR GROUP IS!

If an **AMBULANCE** is required:

TELEPHONE: 999

STATE:
- **AMBULANCE REQUIRED**
- **YOUR NAME**
- **BUILDING LOCATION**
- **NAME(S) AND AGE(S) OF PERSONS ILL OR INJURED**
- **NATURE OF ILLNESS OR INJURY**

<date>

© Health and Safety Executive

FIRE

\<XX\> YOUTH CENTRE
INSTRUCTIONS TO ALL STAFF
IF YOU DISCOVER A FIRE

1 Immediately RAISE THE WARNING by operating the nearest fire alarm, then dial 999 to inform the fire service of the location of the fire.

2 Attack the fire with the nearest available fire appliance, but DO NOT REMAIN IN THE BUILDING IF THERE IS IMMEDIATE DANGER TO YOUR LIFE.

ON HEARING THE FIRE ALARM

1 LEAVE THE BUILDING AT ONCE BY THE NEAREST AVAILABLE EXIT – if possible close windows and doors before leaving. Escort any visitors with you from the building.

DO NOT RE-ENTER THE BUILDING FOR ANY REASON until the 'all clear' has been given.

2 Go immediately to the ASSEMBLY POINT which is
\<XX\>.

3 Keep well away from the building.

4 The Fire Warden for the building is:
\<XX\>.

AT ALL TIMES:
- KEEP CALM
- KEEP QUIET
- DO NOT RUSH OR ATTEMPT TO PUSH PAST OTHERS

[date]

Health and Safety
Executive

Five steps to risk assessment

This is a web-friendly version of leaflet INDG163(rev2), revised 06/06

This leaflet aims to help you assess health and safety risks in the workplace

A risk assessment is an important step in protecting your workers and your business, as well as complying with the law. It helps you focus on the risks that really matter in your workplace – the ones with the potential to cause real harm. In many instances, straightforward measures can readily control risks, for example ensuring spillages are cleaned up promptly so people do not slip, or cupboard drawers are kept closed to ensure people do not trip. For most, that means simple, cheap and effective measures to ensure your most valuable asset – your workforce – is protected.

The law does not expect you to eliminate all risk, but you are required to protect people as far as 'reasonably practicable'. This guide tells you how to achieve that with a minimum of fuss.

This is not the only way to do a risk assessment, there are other methods that work well, particularly for more complex risks and circumstances. However, we believe this method is the most straightforward for most organisations.

What is risk assessment?

A risk assessment is simply a careful examination of what, in your work, could cause harm to people, so that you can weigh up whether you have taken enough precautions or should do more to prevent harm. Workers and others have a right to be protected from harm caused by a failure to take reasonable control measures.

Accidents and ill health can ruin lives and affect your business too if output is lost, machinery is damaged, insurance costs increase or you have to go to court. You are legally required to assess the risks in your workplace so that you put in place a plan to control the risks.

© Health and Safety Executive

How to assess the risks in your workplace

Follow the five steps in this leaflet:

Step 1
Identify the hazards

Step 2
Decide who might be harmed and how

Step 3
Evaluate the risks and decide on precautions

Step 4
Record your findings and implement them

Step 5
Review your assessment and update if necessary

Don't overcomplicate the process. In many organisations, the risks are well known and the necessary control measures are easy to apply. You probably already know whether, for example, you have employees who move heavy loads and so could harm their backs, or where people are most likely to slip or trip. If so, check that you have taken reasonable precautions to avoid injury.

If you run a small organisation and you are confident you understand what's involved, you can do the assessment yourself. You don't have to be a health and safety expert.

If you work in a larger organisation, you could ask a health and safety advisor to help you. If you are not confident, get help from someone who is competent. In all cases, you should make sure that you involve your staff or their representatives in the process. They will have useful information about how the work is done that will make your assessment of the risk more thorough and effective. But remember, you are responsible for seeing that the assessment is carried out properly.

When thinking about your risk assessment, remember:

- a **hazard** is anything that may cause harm, such as chemicals, electricity, working from ladders, an open drawer etc;
- the **risk** is the chance, high or low, that somebody could be harmed by these and other hazards, together with an indication of how serious the harm could be.

Step 1
Identify the hazards

First you need to work out how people could be harmed. When you work in a place every day it is easy to overlook some hazards, so here are some tips to help you identify the ones that matter:

- **Walk around** your workplace and look at what could reasonably be expected to cause harm.
- **Ask your employees** or their representatives what they think. They may have noticed things that are not immediately obvious to you.
- **Visit the HSE website** (www.hse.gov.uk). HSE publishes practical guidance on where hazards occur and how to control them. There is much information here on the hazards that might affect your business.
- Alternatively, **call HSE Infoline** (Tel: 0845 345 0055), who will identify publications that can help you, or contact **Workplace Health Connect** (Tel: 0845 609 6006), a free service for managers and staff of small and medium-sized enterprises providing practical advice on workplace health and safety.
- If you are a member of a **trade association**, contact them. Many produce very helpful guidance.
- **Check manufacturers' instructions** or data sheets for chemicals and equipment as they can be very helpful in spelling out the hazards and putting them in their true perspective.
- Have a look back at your **accident and ill-health records** – these often help to identify the less obvious hazards.
- **Remember to think about long-term hazards to health** (eg high levels of noise or exposure to harmful substances) as well as safety hazards.

Step 2
Decide who might be harmed and how

For each hazard you need to be clear about who might be harmed; it will help you identify the best way of managing the risk. That doesn't mean listing everyone by name, but rather identifying groups of people (eg 'people working in the storeroom' or 'passers-by').

In each case, identify how they might be harmed, ie what type of injury or ill health might occur. For example, 'shelf stackers may suffer back injury from repeated lifting of boxes'.

Remember:

- some workers have particular requirements, eg new and young workers, new or expectant mothers and people with disabilities may be at particular risk. Extra thought will be needed for some hazards;
- cleaners, visitors, contractors, maintenance workers etc, who may not be in the workplace all the time;
- members of the public, if they could be hurt by your activities;
- if you share your workplace, you will need to think about how your work affects others present, as well as how their work affects your staff – talk to them; and
- ask your staff if they can think of anyone you may have missed.

Step 3
Evaluate the risks and decide on precautions

Having spotted the hazards, you then have to decide what to do about them. The law requires you to do everything 'reasonably practicable' to protect people from harm. You can work this out for yourself, but the easiest way is to compare what you are doing with good practice.

There are many sources of good practice – **HSE's website** (www.hse.gov.uk), **HSE Infoline** (Tel: 0845 345 0055) and **Workplace Health Connect** (Tel: 0845 609 6006) will all help.

So first, look at what you're already doing, think about what controls you have in place and how the work is organised. Then compare this with the good practice and see if there's more you should be doing to bring yourself up to standard. In asking yourself this, consider:

- Can I get rid of the hazard altogether?
- If not, how can I control the risks so that harm is unlikely?

When controlling risks, apply the principles below, if possible in the following order:

- try a less risky option (eg switch to using a less hazardous chemical);
- prevent access to the hazard (eg by guarding);
- organise work to reduce exposure to the hazard (eg put barriers between pedestrians and traffic);
- issue personal protective equipment (eg clothing, footwear, goggles etc); and
- provide welfare facilities (eg first aid and washing facilities for removal of contamination).

Improving health and safety need not cost a lot. For instance, placing a mirror on a dangerous blind corner to help prevent vehicle accidents is a low-cost precaution considering the risks. Failure to take simple precautions can cost you a lot more if an accident does happen.

Involve staff, so that you can be sure that what you propose to do will work in practice and won't introduce any new hazards.

Step 4
Record your findings and implement them

Putting the results of your risk assessment into practice will make a difference when looking after people and your business.

Writing down the results of your risk assessment, and sharing them with your staff, encourages you to do this. If you have fewer than five employees you do not have to write anything down, though it is useful so that you can review it at a later date if, for example, something changes.

When writing down your results, keep it simple, for example 'Tripping over rubbish: bins provided, staff instructed, weekly housekeeping checks', or 'Fume from welding: local exhaust ventilation used and regularly checked'.

We do not expect a risk assessment to be perfect, but it must be suitable and sufficient. You need to be able to show that:

- a proper check was made;
- you asked who might be affected;
- you dealt with all the significant hazards, taking into account the number of people who could be involved;
- the precautions are reasonable, and the remaining risk is low; and
- you involved your staff or their representatives in the process.

There is a template at the end of this leaflet that you can print off and use.

If, like many businesses, you find that there are quite a lot of improvements that you could make, big and small, don't try to do everything at once. Make a plan of action to deal with the most important things first. Health and safety inspectors acknowledge the efforts of businesses that are clearly trying to make improvements.

A good plan of action often includes a mixture of different things such as:

- a few cheap or easy improvements that can be done quickly, perhaps as a temporary solution until more reliable controls are in place;
- long-term solutions to those risks most likely to cause accidents or ill health;
- long-term solutions to those risks with the worst potential consequences;
- arrangements for training employees on the main risks that remain and how they are to be controlled;
- regular checks to make sure that the control measures stay in place; and
- clear responsibilities – who will lead on what action, and by when.

Remember, prioritise and tackle the most important things first. As you complete each action, tick it off your plan.

Step 5
Review your risk assessment and update if necessary

Few workplaces stay the same. Sooner or later, you will bring in new equipment, substances and procedures that could lead to new hazards. It makes sense, therefore, to review what you are doing on an ongoing basis. Every year or so formally review where you are, to make sure you are still improving, or at least not sliding back.

Look at your risk assessment again. Have there been any changes? Are there improvements you still need to make? Have your workers spotted a problem? Have you learnt anything from accidents or near misses? Make sure your risk assessment stays up to date.

When you are running a business it's all too easy to forget about reviewing your risk assessment – until something has gone wrong and it's too late. Why not set a review date for this risk assessment now? Write it down and note it in your diary as an annual event.

During the year, if there is a significant change, don't wait. Check your risk assessment and, where necessary, amend it. If possible, it is best to think about the risk assessment when you're planning your change – that way you leave yourself more flexibility.

© Health and Safety Executive

Some frequently asked questions

What if the work I do tends to vary a lot, or I (or my employees) move from one site to another?
Identify the hazards you can reasonably expect and assess the risks from them. This general assessment should stand you in good stead for the majority of your work. Where you do take on work or a new site that is different, cover any new or different hazards with a specific assessment. You do not have to start from scratch each time.

What if I share a workplace?
Tell the other employers and self-employed people there about any risks your work could cause them, and what precautions you are taking. Also, think about the risks to your own workforce from those who share your workplace.

Do my employees have responsibilities?
Yes. Employees have legal responsibilities to co-operate with their employer's efforts to improve health and safety (eg they must wear protective equipment when it is provided), and to look out for each other.

What if one of my employee's circumstances change?
You'll need to look again at the risk assessment. You are required to carry out a specific risk assessment for new or expectant mothers, as some tasks (heavy lifting or work with chemicals for example) may not be appropriate. If an employee develops a disability then you are required to make reasonable adjustments. People returning to work following major surgery may also have particular requirements. If you put your mind to it, you can almost always find a way forward that works for you and your employees.

What if I have already assessed some of the risks?
If, for example, you use hazardous chemicals and you have already assessed the risks to health and the precautions you need to take under the Control of Substances Hazardous to Health Regulations (COSHH), you can consider them 'checked' and move on.

Getting help

If you get stuck, don't give up. There is a wealth of information available to help you. More information about legal requirements and standards can be found on our website at: www.hse.gov.uk, and in particular in our publications (available from HSE Books):

An introduction to health and safety: Health and safety in small businesses Leaflet INDG259(rev1) HSE Books 2003 (single copy free)

Essentials of health and safety at work (Fourth edition) HSE Books 2006 ISBN 0 7176 6179 2

Help is also available from Workplace Health Connect, a free service for managers and staff of small and medium-sized enterprises that provides practical advice on workplace health and safety. Tel: 0845 609 6006
Website: www.workplacehealthconnect.co.uk

Company name:

Date of risk assessment:

Step 1
What are the hazards?

Spot hazards by:

- walking around your workplace;
- asking your employees what they think;
- visiting the 'Your industry areas of the HSE website or calling HSE Infoline;
- calling the Workplace Health Connect Adviceline or visiting their website;
- checking manufacturers' instructions;
- contacting your trade association.

Don't forget long-term health hazards.

Step 2
Who might be harmed and how?

Identify groups of people. Remember:

- some workers have particular needs;
- people who may not be in the workplace all the time;
- members of the public;
- if you share your workplace think about how your work affects others present.

Say how the hazard could cause harm.

Step 3
What are you already doing?

List what is already in place to reduce the likelihood of harm or make any harm less serious.

Step 4
How will you put the assessment into action?

Remember to prioritise. Deal with those hazards that are high-risk and have serious consequences first.

Action   Action   Done
by whom   by whom

What further action is necessary?

You need to make sure that you have reduced risks 'so far as is reasonably practicable'. An easy way of doing this is to compare what you are already doing with good practice. If there is a difference, list what needs to be done.

Step 5 Review date:

- Review your assessment to make sure you are still improving, or at least not sliding back.
- If there is a significant change in your workplace, remember to check your risk assessment and, where necessary, amend it.

160

© Health and Safety Executive

**Health and Safety
Executive**

Further information

HSE priced and free publications are available by mail order from HSE Books,
PO Box 1999, Sudbury, Suffolk CO10 2WA Tel: 01787 881165 Fax: 01787 313995
Website: www.hsebooks.co.uk (HSE priced publications are also available from
bookshops and free leaflets can be downloaded from HSE's website:
www.hse.gov.uk/pubns)

For information about health and safety ring HSE's Infoline Tel: 0845 345 0055
Fax: 0845 408 9566 Textphone: 0845 408 9577 e-mail: hse.infoline@natbrit.com
or write to HSE Information Services, Caerphilly Business Park, Caerphilly
CF83 3GG.

**This leaflet contains notes on good practice which are not compulsory but
which you may find helpful in considering what you need to do.**

This leaflet is available in priced packs of 10 from HSE Books,
ISBN 0 7176 6189 X. Single free copies are also available from HSE Books.

Health & Safety in buildings Calendar

\<Group Name\>

This record relates to
\<Premises\>

December 2012

Health & Safety Calendar and Guide for Managing Buildings

This booklet is intended to provide lead workers and all staff working in buildings with a brief guide to some of the regular health and safety related tasks they are responsible for.

It does not constitute a statement of policy, nor does it pretend to include all the things that staff will be required to deal with in managing buildings and meeting their obligations under health and safety legislation and regulations.

Managing health and safety can be a complex business, especially in shared premises that may have a number of user groups and a lack of clear information about exactly who is responsible for what.

In any situation where staff or volunteers are delivering work with young people, there is a responsibility to ensure the environment and activities do not pose an unnecessary risk to young people, staff or volunteers.

Most health and safety obligations can be met through the systematic assessment and recording of risks and the steps taken to minimise them.

The inclusion of a task in a particular month is only a suggestion. Periodic health and safety tasks can be carried out when contracts and availability of staff and resources dictate. The schedule of work at the back of this document gives the frequency of some inspections, tests and services. Providing the intervals are used, the point in the year where the task is carried out is not important.

This guide will provide prompts to ensure regular checks are made, and will provide some consistency in the way checks are recorded. The lists are not complete – please add any other regular checks which your building requires in the space provided.

Health and Safety Calendar and Guidance

January		Date	Checked by
Task	**Programme risk assessment** (termly)		
Action			
Task	**Fire drill** (3 monthly)		
Action			
Task	**Test fire alarm** (3 monthly)		
Action			
Task	**Fire extinguishers – visual check** (monthly)		
Action			
Task	**Plan local health and safety training** (annually)		
Action			
Task	**Test 1 emergency light**		
Action			
Task	**Check first aid box and refill**		
Action			
Task			
Action			

Health and Safety Calendar and Guidance

February		Date	Checked by
Task	**Test 1 fire alarm break glass point**		
Action			
Task	**Test 1 emergency light**		
Action			
Task	**Fire extinguishers – visual check (monthly)**		
Action			
Task			
Action			
Task			
Action			
Task			
Action			
Task			
Action			
Task			
Action			

Health and Safety Calendar and Guidance

March		Date	Checked by
Task	**Test 1 fire alarm break glass point**		
Action			
Task	**Test 1 emergency light**		
Action			
Task	**Fire extinguishers – visual check (monthly)**		
Action			
Task			
Action			
Task			
Action			
Task			
Action			
Task			
Action			
Task			
Action			

Health and Safety Calendar and Guidance

April		Date	Checked by
Task	**Fire drill (3 monthly)**		
Action			
Task	**Programme risk assessment (termly)**		
Action			
Task	**Fire alarm test (3 monthly)**		
Action			
Task	**Test 1 emergency light**		
Action			
Task	**Fire extinguishers – visual check (monthly)**		
Action			
Task			
Action			
Task			
Action			
Task			
Action			

Health and Safety Calendar and Guidance

May		Date	Checked by
Task	**Test 1 fire alarm break glass point**		
Action			
Task	**Test 1 emergency light**		
Action			
Task	**Fire extinguishers – visual check (monthly)**		
Action			
Task			
Action			
Task			
Action			
Task			
Action			
Task			
Action			
Task			
Action			

Health and Safety Calendar and Guidance

June		Date	Checked by
Task	**Test 1 fire alarm break glass point**		
Action			
Task	**Test 1 emergency light**		
Action			
Task	**Fire extinguishers – visual check (monthly)**		
Action			
Task			
Action			
Task			
Action			
Task			
Action			
Task			
Action			
Task			
Action			

Health and Safety Calendar and Guidance

July		Date	Checked by
Task	**Building risk assessment (annual)**		
Action			
Task	**Test 1 fire alarm break glass point**		
Action			
Task	**Test 1 emergency light**		
Action			
Task	**Fire extinguishers – visual check (monthly)**		
Action			
Task	**Update inventory (annual)**		
Action			
Task			
Action			
Task			
Action			
Task			
Action			

Health and Safety Calendar and Guidance

August		Date	Checked by
Task	**Test 1 fire alarm break glass point**		
Action			
Task	**PAT test all portable electrical equipment (as required)**		
Action			
Task	**Test 1 emergency light**		
Action			
Task	**Fire extinguishers – visual check**		
Action			
Task	**Update and circulate evacuation procedure (include disabled people) (annual)**		
Action			
Task	**Deep clean of ventilation and extraction equipment (annual)**		
Action			
Task			
Action			
Task			
Action			

Health and Safety Calendar and Guidance

September		Date	Checked by
Task	**Fire drill (3 monthly)**		
Action			
Task	**Programme risk assessment (termly)**		
Action			
Task	**Test 1 emergency light**		
Action			
Task	**Fire alarm test (3 monthly)**		
Action			
Task	**Fire extinguishers – visual check (monthly)**		
Action			
Task	**Distribute new annual consent forms**		
Action			
Task			
Action			
Task			
Action			

Health and Safety Calendar and Guidance

October		Date	Checked by
Task	**Test 1 fire alarm break glass point**		
Action			
Task	**Test 1 emergency light**		
Action			
Task	**Fire extinguishers – visual check (monthly)**		
Action			
Task	**Ask staff and volunteers for health and safety training needs (annual)**		
Action			
Task			
Action			
Task			
Action			
Task			
Action			
Task			
Action			

Health and Safety Calendar and Guidance

November		Date	Checked by
Task	**Test 1 fire alarm break glass point**		
Action			
Task	**Test 1 emergency light**		
Action			
Task	**Fire extinguishers – visual check (monthly)**		
Action			
Task			
Action			
Task			
Action			
Task			
Action			
Task			
Action			
Task			
Action			

Health and Safety Calendar and Guidance

December		Date	Checked by
Task	**Ensure fire extinguishers serviced in last 12 months (annually)**		
Action			
Task	**Ensure fire alarm has been serviced in last 12 months (annually)**		
Action			
Task	**Ensure gas appliances have been serviced in last 12 months and certificates are available (annually)**		
Action			
Task			
Action			
Task			
Action			
Task			
Action			
Task			
Action			
Task			
Action			

Health and Safety related tasks
Schedule of work

Frequency	Tasks	Comments
Each session	Visual check of venue to ensure there are no hazards.	Do this even in a building you know well.
	Visual check of equipment to ensure it is fit for purpose.	
Each month	Test 1 emergency light fitting.	Do them all over the year.
	Test 1 fire alarm break glass point.	Do them all over the year.
	Visual check of fire extinguishers.	
Every 3 months	Test fire alarm.	Vary the time and day.
	Fire drill.	Vary the time and day, and learn from what happens.
Every term	Programme risk assessment.	If your programme is termly.
Annual	Update and circulate evacuation procedure.	Ensure everyone understands it.
	Deep clean of ventilation and extraction equipment.	
	Update building risk assessment.	More often if anything changes.
	Update inventory.	New equipment should be added when it arrives.
	Collate health & safety training needs of staff and volunteers.	
	Identify suitable health & safety training .	
	Fire extinguishers serviced.	Each appliance must be stickered.
	Gas appliances serviced and certificated.	Certificate must be available.
	Fire and intruder alarm serviced.	
	Portable appliance testing carried out and recorded.	As per schedule.
	Emergency lighting serviced.	
	First aid box checked & refilled.	
Every 3 years	Full electrical inspection.	

Electrical Safety
Portable Appliance Testing (PAT) – Frequency of Inspections

The frequency of safety testing for electrical appliances depends on the nature of the equipment and its location and use.

Equipment that is used in a youth centre, by young people, and is moved regularly, will need to be tested more often than office equipment that is never moved.

The testing frequencies given are a minimum. Where equipment looks in poor condition, or has been damaged, it should be inspected and tested prior to being used.

Portable electrical equipment can be classified under two headings: Earthed (Class I) and Double Insulated (Class II).

Most high-powered equipment will be Class I. This includes kettles, water heaters, vacuum cleaners, power tools, desk lamps, fans, floor polishers, extension leads, gardening equipment and toasters. Equipment that has a metal frame that you can touch will normally be Class I, and will be earthed through the mains cable.

Lower power equipment, and items that have a plastic body, will normally be Class II. This includes portable stereos, some computer equipment, small desk lamps, televisions, video and DVD players, and set-top boxes. Class II equipment does not have a separate earth lead, so there will only be two cables connected inside the plug.

Class I equipment that is subject to heavy use and regularly moved should be inspected and tested at least every year. This is equipment that is used in youth centres with young people.

Class II equipment that is subject to heavy use and moved regularly should be inspected and tested at least every two years. This is equipment that is used in youth centres with young people.

Class I equipment that is subject to light use, is looked after and not moved regularly should be inspected and tested at least every two years. This is equipment in offices and non-public parts of premises.

Class II equipment that is subject to light use, is looked after and is not moved regularly should be inspected and tested at least every four years. This is equipment in non-public parts of premises.

© Somerset Youth and Community Service 2013

Medical Consent Form Sample

<Name of Organisation>
<Address of Organisation>

Part A: Confidential medical questionnaire

<Name of trip or activity>		
Young person's name:		**Date of birth:**
Parent, guardian or next of kin **Full name:** **Address:** **Emergency contact numbers:** **Home:** **Work:** **Mobile:**		**Doctor's name:** **Address:** **Telephone:** **NHS No:**

Has your son or daughter had any of the following?	YES	NO
Asthma/bronchitis		
Sight/hearing disabilities		
Heart condition		
Fits, fainting or blackouts		
Severe headaches		
Diabetes		
Allergies to any known drugs		
Any other allergies, e.g. material, food, medicine, pollen, dust		
Other illness or disability		
Recent bed wetting		
Sleep walking		
Travel sickness		

If the answer to any of the questions overleaf is YES please give details here:

	YES	NO
Has your son or daughter been vaccinated against tetanus in the last 10 years?		
Has your son or daughter received medical or surgical treatment of any kind from either your family doctor or hospital during the past three months?		
Has your son or daughter been given specific medical advice to following an emergency?		
If the answer to either of the 2 questions above is YES please give the details here (including dosage of any medicine):		
Has your son or daughter received instructions on administering his/her own medication?		

Part B: Certification

I consent to my son or daughter receiving medical care considered necessary and in his or her best interests by the medical authorities during the **<Name of Activity>**

Signed: Date:

Name:

Relationship to young person:

Note: If you would like to discuss any medical matter with the youth worker please call **<Insert Name and Number>**

© Somerset Youth and Community Service 2013

Appendix 27

Minibus Travel Risk Assessment Sample

<Name of Organisation> Minibus Travel Risk Assessment	Written by: <Name of Writer>	Date:	Next review date:			
What is the hazard?	What will be done to control the risk?	What further action is recommended?	By whom?	Date action due	Date action done	
Breakdown	Minibus hired from reputable firm. Check minibus to ensure it is in roadworthy condition before setting out. If breakdown occurs, if possible move minibus to side of road and supervise young people on verge ensuring they are a safe distance from the side of the road. Staff have parental contact details if needed (lateness, change of plan, cancellation). Minibus has breakdown cover.				
Accident	Ensure minibus is in roadworthy condition and only driven by driver who is competent and experienced driving minibuses. Ensure all passengers and driver wear seatbelts. Stick to main roads for journey as far as possible. Ensure no bags are stored in the aisle so that the aisle is kept clear. Minibus has breakdown cover. Minibus has fire extinguisher and first aid box. Staff have parent contact numbers in case of accident. Staff have medical information and medical consent if treatment is needed. Staff have charged mobile phone(s).				
Getting lost	Route planned and noted before trip. Stick to main roads where possible.				

What is the hazard?	What will be done to control the risk?	What further action is recommended?	By whom?	Date action due	Date action done
Distracting the driver	• Ensure one staff member supervises young people in the rear of the minibus. • Only known and trusted young people allowed to sit in the front seats. • Behaviour ground rules agreed by young people before start of journey.				
Travel sickness	• Information about whether or not young people get travel sick asked before the journey. • Sick bags and cleaning materials on the minibus.				
Driver fatigue	• Breaks planned in journey where necessary. • Driver will get good night's sleep the night before the journey. • Driver knows it's OK to take a break if needed.				
Breaks in the journey – young people getting lost or behaving badly	• Journey breaks kept to a minimum. • Young people have staff mobile phone numbers. • Staff have young people's mobile phone numbers. • Young people know where they are allowed and not allowed to go. • Young people know when to be back at the bus. • Behaviour ground rules agreed by young people before the trip. • Young people agree not to talk to strangers and are aware of 'stranger danger' and to inform staff of any concerns immediately.				

Please now pass this assessment to the Chair of the Management Committee for approval

Name of Chair		Date:	Signature:

© Somerset Youth and Community Service 2013

SOMERSET County Council

181

Appendix 28

Residential Risk Assessment Sample

<Name of Organisation> residential trip to <Name of Centre>	Written by: <Name of Writer>	Date:	Next review date:

What is the hazard?	What will be done to control the risk?	What further action is recommended?	By whom?	Date action due	Date action done
Emergency – accident, incident, illness	• Register of young people in operation. • Parents/carers to be advised of emergency contact details of staff on trip. • Staff ensure they have a record of emergency contact numbers for parents/carers of all those attending. • Staff mobile phones fully charged. • Activity centre staff first aid trained and have first aid kit with them. • Staff have medical forms with information. • Treatment consent gained from parents.				
Loss of personal belongings	• Young people to take responsibility for their belongings and to label them if appropriate. • Young people to be advised not to bring anything of value on the trip or large amounts of money. • Young people advised that rooms are lockable.				

What is the hazard?	What will be done to control the risk?	What further action is recommended?	By whom?	Date action due	Date action done
'Stranger Danger'	• Young people briefed that other people will be on the activity centre site prior to trip. • Young people instructed to contact a member of the staff immediately that any issues causing concern arise. • Young people agree not to talk to strangers. • Young people have mobile numbers of staff.				

Behaviour that may be challenging or anti-social.
 	
Physical or verbal abuse from children and young people.
 	
Risk of injury from things getting thrown or broken, psychological harm, damage to property.
	• Known and trusted young people attending.
	• Staff will be observant of possible triggers for behaviour and where possible avoid them.
	• Staff will promote positive behaviour.
	• Staff are capable and confident in dealing with young people.
	• Staff know young people and have positive relationship with them.
	• Parental consent forms, which state acceptable behaviour, have been signed.
	• Young people who seriously misbehave will be taken home (parents or volunteer to collect).
	• Ground rules and consequences concerning behaviour have been discussed and all young people have signed up to them before the trip, including:
	  o Not leaving the site.
	  o Politeness to the public and activity centre staff.
	  o Doing as activity centre staff and youth club staff ask.
	  o No violence, bullying, name calling, sexual behaviour or consumption of drugs or alcohol.
	  o Smoking only in designated areas at agreed times.
	  o Staying in rooms after lights out.
	  o Telling staff if anyone has a problem.
	  o No valuables to be bought along.
	  o Keep to the timetable.
	  o Respect the site.				

What is the hazard?	What will be done to control the risk?	What further action is recommended?	By whom?	Date action due	Date action done
Slipping/tripping/falling at the activity centre Accident at activity centre	• Follow recommended pathways/routes around the activity centre. • Follow health and safety guidance as issued by activity centre staff on arrival. • Follow all health and safety notices. • Young people will be asked to follow the safety advice of activity centre instructors and youth club staff. • Young people advised on appropriate footwear & clothing prior to visit. • Young people advised on, and signed up to, appropriate behaviour before trip. • Staff members trained in first aid. • Medical or first aid centre on site.				
Young people getting lost/separated or not back at meeting point at agreed time	• Young people may be unsupervised for short periods in the evening at the activity centre. Young people will agree a behaviour contract for unsupervised time. • Young people to have staff mobile numbers and staff to have as many numbers of young people as possible. • Young people agree not to go off individually throughout the day/evening. • Do not allow other young people to go looking for missing peers. • In the event of a missing young person alert activity centre staff.				

What is the hazard?	What will be done to control the risk?	What further action is recommended?	By whom?	Date action due	Date action done
Hazards with accommodation – fire, accidents, allergies	• Ensure young people are aware of the fire evacuation procedures. • Young people told not to run on stairs or in corridors. • Ensure activity centre staff are aware of any diet and medical issues. • Young people are aware of the location of youth club staff and duty activity centre staff in the event of an emergency. • Young people are advised where they can smoke at the activity centre. Ensure no smoking in the building.				
Young people in distress or behaving badly at night	• Young people agree to ground rules prior to trip. • Young people know where staff are sleeping, staff have list of which young people are in which rooms. • Rooms and bathrooms are single gender only. • All young people in their rooms by 11.00 and lights out by 11.30 pm. • Youth club staff will do a final check at 11.30 to ensure everyone is in their own room. • Youth club staff will not go to bed until young people are quiet and settled in their rooms. • A night rota for youth club staff will be drawn up. If staff are kept awake all night they can be given down time during activities to catch up on sleep. • All staff know how to contact activity centre duty staff.				

Please now pass this assessment to the Chair of the Management Committee for approval

Name of Chair		Date:		Signature:	

© Somerset Youth and Community Service 2013

185

Visit Consent Form Sample

<Club Name> <Address> <Phone number>	<Club Logo>

Visit Consent Form
For young people aged under 18

<Date and Proposed Visit or Activity>

Dear Parent or Carer,

{Give information on the following:

- *Name of visit or activity*
- *Date*
- *Venue/destination*
- *Details of activities to be undertaken (particularly if they are adventurous or hazardous)*
- *Details of accommodation (if needed)*
- *Staff information and who to contact in case of emergency*
- *Who else is going in the group (age and gender)*
- *Departure place and time*
- *Return place and time*
- *Cost (including how to pay)*
- *Transport arrangements*
- *Kit list*
- *Date by which reply is needed and who to send it to*

Keep in the information below. Give out two copies – one to be returned and one for parents/carers to keep – Mark them clearly!}

Conduct: In order for all young people to have an enjoyable time there have to be certain ground rules that must be followed at all times. These include participants refraining from any behaviour that places a young person, member of staff or member of the public at risk (for example bullying, vandalism, the misuse of drugs or alcohol). We ask for your support in ensuring these rules are adhered to.

Photography: We may take individual or group photographs of young people taking part in activities that may then be used for displays, in publications we produce or on selected websites. We may also make video or webcam recordings of activities and take photographs or film footage in which young people may appear, sometimes named in local or national newspapers or on television. If you have any objections please state them in writing in the box provided.

Please state any objection:
PLEASE LEAVE BLANK IF YOU HAVE NO OBJECTION

Additional information: If there are any other issues that you believe staff should be aware of (e.g. related to faith or religion) please note them below:

Medical Information: Please give us any medical information that you think may be relevant (for example, medical conditions, emotional issues, current medications or allergies):

I have read, fully understood and am satisfied with the details supplied about the above-mentioned activities and agree to my daughter or son taking part in them. I know of no medical reason why they should not participate and I am happy with arrangements outlined regarding photography and behaviour.

Parent or carer's name:	Parent or carer's signature:	Young person's name and date of birth:

Emergency Contact Details

Name of parent/guardian:	
Address:	
Emergency telephone:	Daytime: Evening: Mobile:

Alternative emergency contact should parents/guardians not be available:

Name:		Relationship to child:	
Address:			
Telephone:	Daytime: Evening: Mobile		

© Somerset Youth and Community Service 2013

Appendix 30

Youth Club General Activities Risk Assessment Sample

<Name of Organisation> Routine Activities Risk Assessment	Written by:	Date:	Next review date:

Who could be harmed, and how?	What is already being done to control the risks?	What further action is recommended to reduce risks?	Action by whom?	Date action due	Date action done
Behaviour that may be challenging. Physical or verbal abuse from children and young people attending. Risk of injury from direct physical contact and through things getting thrown or broken; psychological harm; damage to property.	• Ground rules agreed with young people and displayed. • Ensure staff are capable and confident in dealing with young people (ensure appropriate skills, knowledge and experience). • Make sure staff are aware of guidelines to ensure safety of staff, young people and other people. Staff and volunteers will be observant of possible triggers for behaviour and where possible avoid them.	Key staff to have appropriate training		Ongoing	

Who could be harmed, and how?	What is already being done to control the risks?	What further action is recommended to reduce risks?	Action by whom?	Date action due	Date action done
Anti-social behaviour – all, members of public	• Ground rules and sanctions agreed with young people and displayed. • Staff promote positive behaviour and try to divert young people to positive activities and groups. • Young people informed that they cannot bring or use alcohol/non-prescriptive drugs. • Appropriate staff supervision levels for the number and behaviour of young people. • Behaviour policy and re-admittance procedure (if young people are banned) are in place and known by staff and young people. • Young people will be sent home if their misbehaviour is serious (or if they bring alcohol/drugs etc. to centre).				
Playing pool – personal injury from cues and flying balls	• Staff monitor the use of the pool table and its equipment and inform the young people of safe use of it. • Accident/incident procedure and recording in place.				
Drug (including alcohol) use – staff, young people, members of the public	• Create awareness of the dangers of alcohol and drugs. • If worker suspects child/young person has been using drugs or alcohol they ask them to go home. • Follow policy and inform line management as necessary.				

Who could be harmed, and how?	What is already being done to control the risks?	What further action is recommended to reduce risks?	Action by whom?	Date action due	Date action done
Emergency – accident, incident, illness	• Young people and their parents/carers informed of contact numbers of staff on premises and youth club number. • Staff try to ensure they have a record of emergency contact numbers for parents/carers of all young people. • Staff are first aid trained and have first aid kit with them. • Staff have access to a phone if an ambulance or a parent's presence is needed.				
Noise – from karaoke, stereo, general talking and playing etc.	• Staff to monitor the volume of the stereo and karaoke and reduce it when necessary. • Staff to ensure that young people know what is acceptable and are encouraged to keep within that limit.				
Art & craft activities – damage to clothing; injury to skin/allergic reaction.	• Appropriate supervision from staff and volunteers. • Young people made aware of risks. • Where possible – materials are washable and non-irritant. • Safety scissors provided. • First aid provision on site. • All members complete consent forms to attend the club listing medical issues.				

Who could be harmed, and how?	What is already being done to control the risks?	What further action is recommended to reduce risks?	Action by whom?	Date action due	Date action done
Use of kitchen – burns, cuts, hygiene	<ul><li>Kitchen door to be left open at all times unless cooking is taking place with a member of staff.</li><li>The serving hatch should be left open at all times.</li><li>If cooking is taking place, no tuck to be served.</li><li>Microwave and cooker only to be used under supervision of responsible adult.</li><li>Young people only to use kettle while supervised, or staff confident it is safe for them to do so.</li><li>When microwave, cooker or kettle in use, maximum of 2 young people allowed in kitchen with staff.</li><li>Young people only to use sharp knives under supervision.</li><li>Sharp knives to be stored safely in drawer in kitchen.</li><li>Sharp knives not to be removed from the kitchen area.</li><li>All food preparation to be supervised by staff with a food hygiene certificate.</li><li>Cleaning and hygiene standards to be maintained.</li></ul>				

© Somerset Youth and Community Service 2013

Who could be harmed, and how?	What is already being done to control the risks?	What further action is recommended to reduce risks?	Action by whom?	Date action due	Date action done
Team games – softball, team building etc., non hazardous	• Adequate staff supervision of activity. • Staff ensure young people understand rules of the games and safety procedures. • Playing area is free from trip hazards and sharp edges. • Staff check equipment prior to use. • Staff ensure that area is big enough for activity and numbers of young people. • First aid kit on site.				
Damage to property/equipment – financial risk, risk of injury through using damaged equipment or equipment malfunctioning	• Staff to inform young people of appropriate and safe use of equipment, consequences of wilful damage and are encouraged to report to staff if they notice anything is broken. • Accident/incident procedure and recording in place. • Staff check safety of equipment before each session and repair/dispose of any damaged equipment.				

Who could be harmed, and how?	What is already being done to control the risks?	What further action is recommended to reduce risks?	Action by whom?	Date action due	Date action done
Lone Working – staff, intruder, child protections	• Staff do not work with individual young people alone when building is empty. • Staff let chair of management committee or worker in charge know if they are working alone. • Internal front door has lock and keypad on it. • Staff do not put self in danger through risky practice – climbing ladders etc. when working alone. • Staff have personal support plan when working at night.	At end of sessions at night other staff wait until building is locked and secure.			

Please now pass this assessment to the Chair of the Management Committee for approval.

	Date:	Chair's comments:
Name of Chair:		
Signature:		

Advert Sample

Salary £**<XX,XXX>** per annum, pro rata (£**<X.XX>** per hour)

Youth Worker-in-Charge/Youth Worker/Youth Support Worker *{delete as appropriate}*.

A vacancy exists at **<Name of Organisation>** for a Youth Worker-in-Charge/Youth Worker/Youth Support Worker *{delete as appropriate}*.

1 x 3 hours a week Youth Worker-in-Charge/Youth Worker/Youth Support Worker *{delete as appropriate}* post in <Name of Town>, currently <Day of the Week> evenings

<Name of Organisation> is a vibrant youth club with many facilities for young people. Staff provide a fun and varied programme. Past programmes include work about **<Details of Programme – for example stress, sport, healthy eating and alcohol>**. You will be delivering alongside an enthusiastic youth work team led by **<Name of Staff Member in Charge>** who leads the session.

Times of work will be **<Day of the Week>** evenings. Other evening/weekend work may be required.

If you consider yourself a team worker, enjoy working with young people aged 11-19, are motivated, innovative, have energy and are over 18, then we would like to meet you.

For an informal conversation about this post, please contact **<Chair of Management Committee/Staff Member in Charge>** on **<XXXX XXXXXX>**.

For an application pack contact: **<Name, address and telephone number of contact>**.

Closing date for applications: **<Time and Date>**.

Interview date: **<Time and Date>** at **<Name of Organisation>**.

Appendix 32

Application Form Sample

APPLICATION FOR EMPLOYMENT WITH <Name of Organisation>

Please return this form to:
<Name and address of management committee member>

Application for the post of:	
Closing date:	
How did you hear about this job? (Name of publication if advertised):	

PART A: PERSONAL DETAILS (BLOCK CAPITALS PLEASE)

Family Name/Surname	
Previous Name(s)	
Forename(s)	
Known Name: (If different from forename)	
Preferred Title: (E.g. Mr, Mrs, Miss, Ms, Dr)	
Current Address: (Please include postcode)	
National Insurance Number:	
Preferred Contact Telephone Number:	
Alternative Telephone Number: (If available)	
Email Address: (If preferred method of communication & in regular use)	
Date of Birth:	

PART B: PRESENT (OR MOST RECENT) EMPLOYER

Name and Address of Employer:	
Job Title:	

Start Date:		Notice required or date left:	
Salary:		If part-time, please give hours per week:	

Please give details of your main tasks and responsibilities – and, if applicable, your reason for leaving:

Please explain why you are applying for this post:

PART C: EMPLOYMENT HISTORY (MOST RECENT FIRST)

Please give as much relevant information as possible. For posts working with children and vulnerable adults, you must give your **full** employment history from when you left school/higher education and explain any gaps in your employment and include dates. Please include any time spent employed as a volunteer.

Name & Address of Employer	Dates From/To (MM/YY)	Job Role	Final Salary and Reason for Leaving

PART D: ACADEMIC, PROFESSIONAL AND VOCATIONAL QUALIFICATIONS

Exams Passed (Level) Qualifications & Memberships (Most Recent First)	Grade and Date Achieved*	Name of Educational Establishment and/or Professional or Awarding Body

*For posts working with children/vulnerable adults you must provide all dates.

PART E: TRAINING/CONTINUING PROFESSIONAL DEVELOPMENT

Please give details of relevant training/development activities.		
Training Course and Organiser or Development Activity	Time spent	Outcome – Grade Achieved (Where applicable)

PART F: PERSONAL STATEMENT

You may continue on a separate sheet if you need to.

Key Competencies, Knowledge and Skills: Referring to the person specification, provide examples of how you have demonstrated the key competencies and the knowledge and skill requirements for this role. You may use experience gained from within and/or outside the workplace to provide these examples. (We recommend that you use the different headings on the person specification as a starting point.)

Personal Attributes: Please describe ways in which you have demonstrated the personal attributes required for this post, as outlined in the person specification.

PART G: SUPPLEMENTARY INFORMATION

Personal Transport: For posts which involve travel away from normal place of work:

Are you willing and able to travel to meet the requirements of the post? Yes ☐ No ☐

Please provide details of any current motoring convictions, disqualifications or penalty points, with dates and reasons and/or any difficulties you foresee concerning travel:

Sickness Declaration: Please supply information about sickness absence in the past 2 years:

Number of days sickness:	Number of occasions:

Any explanatory comments you feel are relevant:

Positive About Disability: We welcome applications from people with disabilities. Wherever possible we will make reasonable adjustments to enable a person with a disability to access the application and appointment process fairly.

Do you consider yourself to have a disability? Yes ☐ No ☐

If "yes" and you are offered an interview, would you welcome a pre-interview discussion to identify any particular needs that you may have? Yes ☐ No ☐

Disclosure of Criminal Offences:

This post requires a Disclosure Certificate and the Rehabilitation of Offenders Act does not apply in this case. Therefore, please give details, including dates and places, of any 'spent' convictions, cautions and bind-overs. Please also detail if you are on List 99, the PoCA List, disqualified from working with children or vulnerable adults or subject to sanctions imposed by a regulatory body such as the General Teaching Council or General Social Care Council:

© Somerset Youth and Community Service 2013

PART H: REFERENCES AND DECLARATIONS

References: Please provide the names of two professional referees, both of whom can write with authority about your performance, abilities and competence in a work, voluntary or educational environment. The first reference must be a manager representing your current or most recent employer. References will not be accepted from relations or people who know you solely as a friend. For posts working with children, **all** references will be requested before interview. For other vacancies, if you do not wish your current employer to be contacted prior to interview please tick the box below*.

If you are applying for a post working with children or vulnerable adults:
Your first referee must be a manager representing your current/most recent employer. If this post has not involved working with children or vulnerable adults but a previous post has, that previous employer must be given as your second referee. This applies even if you have done other work in between.

Name of first referee: * ☐	
Job title of referee:	
Name of organisation:	
Dates of employment:	From: / To: /
Address (including postcode):	
Email address if available:	
Daytime telephone number:	
Relationship to you: (e.g. supervisor, tutor)	
Name of second referee:	
Job title of referee:	
Name of organisation:	
Address (including postcode):	
Dates of employment:	From: / To: /
Email address if available:	
Daytime telephone number:	
Relationship to you:	

Declaration:

- I confirm that I am entitled to live and work in the United Kingdom.
- I am willing for this data to be held and processed by **<Name of Organisation>** and to be verified with relevant third parties. This may include previous employers.
- The information on this form is accurate. I understand that providing false information is an offence and may lead to my application being disallowed or, should I be appointed, to my dismissal and, where appropriate, may be referred to the police.

Signed: Date:

Company/Self-Employed Staff Contract Sample

1. Introduction

1.1 This document is formal confirmation of **<Name of Organisation>** (the purchaser)'s intent to enter into contractual arrangements with **<Name of Company/Self-Employed Contractor>** (the provider) to provide **<Type of Service>** service subject to the conditions noted below.

2. Duration of Agreement

2.1 This agreement shall commence on **<Start Date>** and will expire on **<End Date>** unless terminated by either party during that period in accordance with the termination provisions in this agreement.

3. Aim

3.1 This service will provide:

<Name and brief aim of the service>

3.2 Outputs and outcomes:

- The service will offer **<Number of Sessions>** sessions
- Attendance will average **<Number of Attendees>** young people aged 11-19

<Add more information here from specification>

4. Service Delivery

4.1 The provider will be the lead for the delivery of the service as noted in 3.1. Working in partnership with the purchaser, the provider will be responsible for:

- Completing appropriate paperwork to meet the requirements of health and safety, safeguarding and parental consent
- Recruitment of young people
- Securing and paying for a suitable venue
- Liaison with other services as necessary
- Recording sessions using the agreed form and providing quarterly statistical returns to the purchaser

<Add more information here as necessary>

4.2 The provider warrants that its staff are sufficiently competent to perform their duties and, where necessary, hold such qualifications or licences as may be legally required.

4.3 The provider must provide the service in an efficient and professional manner and in accordance with any applicable statutory requirements and relevant policies of the purchaser. For the avoidance of doubt, the provider shall comply fully with the obligations that are imposed upon it by the Safeguarding Vulnerable Groups Act 2006 and shall do so in accordance with the implementation timetable set out in the act or subsequent statutory guidance or regulations.

5. Financial Arrangements

5.1 See Appendix B – Finance Schedule

5.2 The purchaser will raise any query regarding the provider's invoices within 14 days of their date of issue. Payment will be made **<Monthly/Quarterly>** in arrears of the service being provided.

Save for any unresolved issues the purchaser undertakes to settle the account no later than 30 days from the date of invoice.

5.3 The purchaser will pay the provider upon receipt of invoice the amount as agreed for the length of the contract from the agreed start date in section 2.1. This is subject to the service being delivered in a satisfactory way.

5.4 Invoices should be addressed to:

<Name and Address of Treasurer or Chairperson>

5.5 In the event that payments fall overdue, upon giving 7 days' notice in writing to the purchaser, the provider may suspend provision of the services or upon giving 28 days' notice treat the default as a material breach of this contract.

5.6 The provider shall provide the purchaser with copies of its most up to date financial accounts, which have been independently certified and verified. Where certified accounts are not available (for example where the organisation has been trading for less than a year) or further evidence of financial viability is required, other financial information such as group accounts (where the provider is a subsidiary company), profit/loss accounts, business plan or cash flow forecast shall be provided if requested by the purchaser.

5.7 The accounts shall include turnover, balance sheets and a profit and loss account to include any additional notes and any more up to date information available (e.g. interim or draft accounts). The purchaser reserves the right to withdraw from this agreement should information reasonably required not be provided, or where the purchaser has unresolved concerns about the provider's financial situation, such as solvency. In the event of such withdrawal, the provider shall not have any right to compensation.

5.8 The provider shall respond in full to any reasonable queries from the purchaser regarding financial issues during the agreement period. Where the purchaser has reasonable concerns regarding the finances or viability of the provider, which otherwise cannot be resolved, the provider shall be empowered to obtain letters from the accountants, auditors, banks and/or solicitors to confirm that these parties know of no factors that may adversely affect the provider's ability to fulfil their obligations under the agreement.

5.9 Financial accounts will remain confidential and will only be shared, on a professional basis, with internal financial support staff that carry out financial vetting on behalf of the purchaser.

6. Reviews and Monitoring of Service

6.1 A written review of the operation of the agreement by the purchaser and provider will take place every **<three months/six months>** during the agreement period. The review will focus on the operation and finances of the service.

6.2 A review may be called by either party should there be concerns about the service or if any potential changes need to be made to the agreed service.

6.3 If a review indicates to the purchaser that the service is not being performed in accordance with the agreement, the parties shall endeavour to agree an improvement plan. The Dispute Procedure set out below will follow should the matter not be resolved.

6.4 One unannounced visit will be undertaken per year.

7. Transfer or Assignment

7.1 The provider shall not, without the prior written permission of the purchaser, transfer or assign, directly or indirectly, to any person or persons, the whole or part of this agreement without the written consent of the purchaser, except for the hiring of staff in cases of emergency or planned absence, whereupon such consent will not be unreasonably withheld. The provider shall record the use of temporary staff and make such information available to the purchaser during reviews of the service.

8. Data Protection

8.1 The parties will observe their obligations under the Data Protection Act 1998 and associated regulations to ensure full compliance with the law information.

8.2 The provider will maintain appropriate policies on Confidentiality and Security of Information and make these policies available to all its staff with a written record that this has been done.

8.3 Young people's information held in a paper filing system must be kept in lockable, fireproof cabinets and information held within electronic databases should be password protected.

8.4 Young people's information provided by the purchaser shall remain the property of the purchaser and should not be divulged to anyone other than the staff providing the service. In the event of a request directed to the provider from a young person exercising their right to access under the Data Protection Act 1998 the purchaser must be consulted **before** any information is released.

9. Freedom of Information

9.1 The parties to this agreement will comply with any requests for information relating to this service from service users, members of the public and other organisations where disclosure of such information is in the public interest and would not have a detrimental effect on the commercial interests of either party.

9.2 Where a request is made to the provider for information relating to this service the provider will await permission from the purchaser before releasing such information. The purchaser will not unreasonably withhold such permission.

9.3 Where a request is made to the purchaser for information relating to the provider in relation to this agreement, the provider will be consulted before any information is released.

9.4 The purchaser will comply in full with legislation regarding information held by public bodies. The final decision on disclosure or application exemptions to disclosure of information relating to this service will be made by the purchaser in accordance with any such legislation.

10. Intellectual Property

10.1 In this agreement 'Intellectual Property' means any and all the following:

- Registered trade marks
- Unregistered trade marks
- Registered designs
- Copyright

11. Disputes

11.1 The parties to this agreement shall use their best endeavours to resolve by agreement any disputes between them with respect to any matter relating to this agreement.

11.2 Level 1 – Response/Disputes

Either party requests an appointment to discuss the area(s) of concern, which are outlined in writing.

Both parties will meet to discuss the area(s) of concern and endeavour to resolve the issue(s)/complaint(s) agreeing a timetabled action plan.

11.3 Level 2 – Unresolved Action Following Level 1

Either party will bring the matter to the attention of their senior managers.

Either party will write to the other outlining the cause for concern and detailing the steps each party has already taken, and outline the issues that are still unresolved.

Both parties will meet to agree an action plan and timescale.

11.4 Level 3 – Unresolved Action Following Level 2

Either party will write to the other informing them that the service will be suspended whilst the dispute remains unresolved.

12. Termination

12.1 Either party may terminate this agreement by giving not less than **28 days notice** in writing to that effect but subject to the respective rights and liabilities of the parties accrued to the date of such termination.

This clause should only be enforceable if the provider is in breach of contract by providing poor service without remedy through partnership working with the purchaser.

13. Health and Safety

13.1 The provider shall at all times take such precautions as are necessary to protect the health and safety of all persons who may be affected by the provider's provision of the service, and shall comply with the requirements of the Health and Safety at Work Act 1974 and of any other acts, regulations or order pertaining to health and safety at work or any re-enactment thereof.

14. Insurance

14.1 The provider shall maintain the following minimum insurance arrangements:

- Employer's Liability: £5m in respect of any one claim.
- Public liability: £2m in respect of any one claim.

14.2 At the request of the purchaser, the provider shall produce the necessary insurance certificate(s) for inspection.

15. Variation

15.1 Variation to this agreement may only be made in writing and by agreement by the parties.

16. Signatures

16.1 I, the authorised representative of the purchaser agree to the terms and conditions of this agreement.

Signed:

Name:

Designation:

Date:

16.2 I, the authorised representative of the service provider, agree to the terms and conditions under this agreement.

Signed:

Name:

Designation:

Date:

Appendix A: Contact Details

The Service Purchaser

Name:
Designation:
Address:

Telephone:
Email:

The Service Provider

Name:
Designation:
Address:

Telephone:
Email:

Appendix B: Financial Schedule

Overall value of agreement:

<Monthly/quarterly> payment value:

Other financial considerations:

- Income
- Profit
- Etc.

Application Pack Information

\<Name of Organisation\> Information Sheet

\<Name of Organisation\> provides fun, exciting and challenging opportunities for the young people of \<Name of Town/Village\>. The youth club is open \<one/two/three\> nights a week and around \<number\> young people attend each session. \<Name of Organisation\> is a community organisation funded by \<information\> and has a mix of paid staff and volunteers.

The youth club currently runs \<Day(s) of the Week\> evening session(s), which is open from \<Starting to Finishing Time\> for young people aged \<Age Range\>. It also runs a session for young people aged \<Age Range\> on \<Day(s) of the Week\> evenings from \<Opening Times\>. Young people are encouraged to become involved in the management and running of this youth club, including developing a programme of activities and trips.

The youth work team is currently made up of one staff member in charge and \<one/two/three\> youth workers/volunteers.

What the role involves:
\<Name of Organisation\> needs a new member of staff who is able to communicate, work alongside, enthuse, support, challenge and believe in young people. To draw out the best in young people, laugh with them, enable them to develop and grow and to encourage them to play an active role in their community.

The youth workers are there to help support young people and can provide information, advice and support on a range of issues that affect their lives. Youth workers can also provide access to training for young people so they can develop skills and ideas for themselves.

What skills are needed?
The ability to adapt the personal skills you have developed over the years and employ them in work with 11-19 year-old groups. Remembering your own adolescence may be a useful starting point, in identifying what support young people require, what energy they have, what questions exist and what a difference a youth worker, as a positive role model and enabler, can have in the lives of adolescents.

What are the rewards?
Apart from the salary, the rewards include: the opportunity to work as a member of a committed and enthusiastic team, support in undertaking training and the opportunity to work with energetic, enthusiastic and committed young people. In undertaking this role there are likely to be several opportunities to try something new for yourself, ranging from outdoor activities to role play, drama or go-karting. There will be lots of times when you will make a positive difference in young people's lives and also, have a lot of fun!

Sample Written Statement of Employment

Name of employer: <Name of Organisation>
Employer's address: <Official Address of Management Committee>

Telephone number: <Telephone Number of Management Committee>
Name of employee: <Employee's Name>
Job title: <Job Title>

1. **Commencement of employment and continuous employment**
   Your employment with **<Name of Organisation>** will begin on **<Start Date>**.

   Your period of continuous employment will begin on **<Start Date>**.

2. **Probation**
   Confirmation of your employment will be subject to the satisfactory completion of a probationary period of **<three/six>** months. During your probationary service, you will be expected to establish your suitability for the job.

3. **Line Management**
   You will be line managed by **<Chairperson of the Management Committee/Staff Member in Charge>**. *{Delete as appropriate, the Staff Member in Charge will be line managed by the Chair; Youth Workers line managed by the Staff Member in Charge.}*

4. **Job description**
   <Enter 'main duties' from job description here>

5. **Job location(s)**
   You will work mainly at the following location:
   <Address of Youth Club>

   Flexibility in terms of location has been agreed.
   You will go on trips and visits with young people when required.

6. **Pay**
   Your rate of pay is £**<XX.XX>** gross per hour. This will be paid monthly in arrears by **<cheque/bank transfer>**. *{Delete as appropriate}*. Your salary will be reviewed on 1 April each year and you will be informed on any rise in salary by 31 April. Any increase will be backdated to 1 April. Annual salary increases are discretionary and not guaranteed.

7. **Hours of work**
   You are employed to work part time.
   Your normal working hours will be **<Number of delivery hours plus portion of management time>** hours per week. *{see below}*
   You will work on the following days: **<Day(s) of the Week>** evening(s).
   You will normally work between the hours of **<Start Time>** and **<Finish Time>**.
   You will occasionally be required to work weekends.

© Somerset Youth and Community Service 2013

The day(s) of the week you are required to work may change according to the needs of **<Name of Organisation>**. You will be given one month's notice of any change.

Your weekly contracted hours include youth work delivery hours (see normal working hours above) and hours for the following:

- Training: 12 hours per year *{this is the equivalent of two days and is recommended}*
- Supervision: 6 hours per year *{this is one hour every two months and is recommended}*
- Staff Meetings: 6 hours per year *{this is two hours each term and is recommended}*

Total management time equals 24 hours per year and your monthly salary includes 2 hours for the above, to be worked in agreement with your manager.

Overtime will not be paid. Working additional hours must be agreed in advance with your line manager and time off in lieu taken.

8. Holidays
You are entitled to 25 days holiday (pro rata) per year.
This excludes public holidays, for which you will receive pro rata paid time off.
Your holiday year begins on 1st April.
Unused entitlement may not be carried forward to the next holiday year.

9. Sickness absence
If you cannot work because of illness, you must inform the Chairperson of the Management Committee as early as possible on the first day and each subsequent day when you are unable to work. Self-certification is allowed for a maximum of 5 days after which a Doctor's Certificate must be provided.

You are entitled to contractual sick pay at your normal rate of pay for a maximum of **<Number of Weeks>** *{recommended 1 week}* (pro rata) for any one period of incapacity. You will be entitled to a maximum of **<Number of Weeks>** *{recommended 4 weeks}* sick pay (pro rata) in any one year. This is subject to the requirements to notify the employer and provide evidence of incapacity. Thereafter, you may be entitled to statutory sick pay.

10. Maternity/Paternity/Adoption Leave
Under the provision of the Employment Rights Act 1996 (as amended by the Employment Act 2002 and regulations there under) eligible employees will be entitled to maternity/paternity/adoption leave.

11. Pension scheme
There is no pension scheme and therefore there is no contracting-out certificate in force for this employment, in England under the Pension Schemes Act 1993, or in Northern Ireland under the Pension Schemes (Northern Ireland) Act 1993.

12. Collective agreements with trade unions
There are no collective agreements with trade unions or other employee groups affecting this employment.

13. Ending the employment
This employment is permanent subject to each party's right to terminate in accordance with the terms of this statement. If you want to leave this employment, you must give **<Number of Weeks>** *{recommended 1 month}* notice. We must give you **<Number of Weeks>** *{recommended 1 month}* notice if we want to end this employment.

14. Disciplinary procedure

It is committee policy that the following procedure should be followed when an employee is being disciplined or dismissed. The procedure provides that in normal cases an employee will be given a series of warnings before discipline or dismissal is contemplated. The stages of the procedure that apply when a disciplinary penalty, e.g. demotion or dismissal, is applied. Matters that may be dealt with under this disciplinary and dismissal procedure include discipline and dismissal for the following reasons:

- misconduct
- sub-standard performance
- harassment or victimisation
- misuse of company facilities, including computer facilities (e.g. email and the internet)
- poor timekeeping
- unauthorised absences

Minor cases of misconduct and most cases of poor performance may be dealt with by informal advice, coaching and counselling. An informal oral warning may be given, which does not count as part of the formal disciplinary procedure. No formal record of this type of warning will be kept. If there is no improvement or the matter is serious enough, you will be invited to a disciplinary meeting at which the matter can be properly discussed. You will be allowed to bring a work colleague or trade union representative to the meeting. The outcome of the meeting will be communicated to you. There are the following possible outcomes:

Oral warning

In the case of minor infringements you may be given a formal oral warning. A note of the oral warning will be kept on your file but will be disregarded for disciplinary purposes after a specified period (e.g. six months). You have the right to appeal against a formal oral warning.

Written warning

If the infringement is more serious or there is no improvement in conduct after a formal oral warning you will be given a formal written warning giving details of the complaint, the improvement or change in behaviour required, the timescale allowed for this, the right of appeal and the fact that a final written warning may be given if there is no sustained satisfactory improvement or change. A copy of the written warning will be kept on file but will be disregarded for disciplinary purposes after a specified period (e.g. 12 months).

Final written warning

Where there is a failure to improve or change behaviour while a prior formal written warning is still in effect, or where the infringement is sufficiently serious, you may be given a final written warning. This will give details of the complaint, warn that failure to improve will lead to dismissal and refer to the right of appeal. The final written warning will be kept on file but will normally be disregarded for disciplinary purposes after a specified period (e.g. 12 months).

Dismissal

If your conduct or performance still fails to improve, the final step will be to contemplate dismissal, or taking action short of dismissal, e.g. demotion. If we are contemplating dismissing you or applying some other disciplinary penalty, we will begin the following procedure:

Step 1: We give you a written statement and call a meeting to discuss the matter

We will set out in writing your alleged conduct, characteristics or other circumstances, which led us to contemplate dismissing or taking disciplinary action against you. We will also set out the basis on which we have made the allegations against you. If possible, we will provide you with copies of any relevant evidence against you. We will invite you to a hearing to discuss the matter.

Step 2: A meeting is held and the employer informs the employee of the outcome
The meeting will take place before any disciplinary action, other than suspension on full pay, is taken. The meeting will be held without undue delay but only when you have had a reasonable opportunity to consider your response to our written statement and any further verbal explanation we may give. You must take all reasonable steps to attend the meeting.
After the meeting we will inform you of our decision and notify you of your right to appeal if you are not satisfied with it.

Step 3: Appeal against the disciplinary decision if necessary
If you wish to appeal you must inform the Chairperson of the Management Committee in writing within a reasonable time.
If you do this, we will invite you to attend a further meeting. You must take all reasonable steps to attend the meeting. If practicable a more senior manager not previously involved in the disciplinary procedure will hear the appeal.
The appeal hearing may take place before or after dismissal or disciplinary action has taken effect. After the appeal hearing we will inform you of our final decision and confirm it in writing as soon as practicable.

Gross misconduct
If, after investigation, it is confirmed that you have committed one of the following offences (the list is not exhaustive), you will normally be dismissed:

- theft
- fraud and deliberate falsification of records
- physical violence
- serious bullying or harassment
- deliberate damage to property
- serious insubordination
- misuse of an organisation's property or name
- bringing the employer into serious disrepute
- serious incapability whilst on duty brought on by alcohol or non-prescription drugs
- serious negligence, which causes or might cause unacceptable loss, damage or injury
- serious infringement of health and safety rules
- serious breach of confidence (subject to the Public Interest (Disclosure) Act 1998)
- inappropriate behaviour with young people

While the alleged gross misconduct is being investigated, you may be suspended, during which time you will be paid. In most cases any decision to dismiss will be taken only after we have fully investigated the matter.

However, in a few cases of gross misconduct we may be justified in dismissing immediately without conducting an investigation. In these cases a two-step procedure will be followed:

Step 1: We give you a written statement
We will give you a written statement setting out the conduct that has resulted in your immediate dismissal and informing you of the right to appeal against the decision to dismiss.

Step 2: Appeal against the decision to dismiss

If you wish to appeal you must inform the Chairperson of the Management Committee. A meeting must be held (in accordance with the general principles set out above). We will then inform you of our decision as soon as possible after the meeting.

General principles applicable to the procedures

The following principles apply to the dismissal procedures set out above:

1. The person who has authority to discipline you in accordance with these procedures is your line manager.
2. You have the right to be accompanied to any meeting by a trade union representative or co-worker.
3. Each step in the procedure will be taken without unreasonable delay and hearings will be held at reasonable times and locations.
4. Meetings will be conducted in a manner that enables both us and you to explain their cases.
5. We will keep records detailing the nature of any breach of disciplinary rules or unsatisfactory performance, your defence or mitigation, the action taken and the reasons for it, whether an appeal was lodged, its outcome and any subsequent developments. We will keep these records confidential.

15. Grievance procedure

It is committee policy to ensure that any employee with a grievance has access to a procedure, which can lead to a speedy resolution of the grievance in a fair manner.

Most routine complaints and grievances are best resolved informally in discussion with your immediate line manager. Where the grievance cannot be resolved informally it will be dealt with under the following procedure:

The standard grievance procedure

Step 1: You give us a written statement of your grievance

You must put your grievance in a written statement and send a copy to the Chairperson of the Management Committee. Where the grievance is against this individual, the matter should be raised with a more senior manager if there is one.

Step 2: A meeting is held and we inform you of the outcome

We will then invite you to attend a meeting to discuss the grievance. The meeting will only take place once you have informed us of the basis for the grievance you have set out in your written statement, and we have had a reasonable opportunity to consider what response to make. You must take all reasonable steps to attend the meeting.

As soon as possible after the meeting we will inform you of the decision taken in response to the grievance and notify you of your right to appeal if you are not satisfied with it.

Step 3: Appeal if necessary

If you then wish to appeal, you must inform us and we will invite you to an appeal hearing. You must take all reasonable steps to attend. If reasonably practicable, a more senior manager who has not been involved in the grievance procedure so far will deal with the appeal. As soon as possible after the hearing, we will inform you of our decision, which will be final.

Raising grievances after you have left the company

If you wish to raise a grievance after you have left the company's employment, you must follow a two-step procedure:

Step 1: You give us a written statement of your grievance
You must put your grievance in a written statement and send a copy to the Chairperson of the Management Committee.

Step 2: We give you a written response
We will write back to you giving our response to the points you have raised.

General principles applicable to the procedures

1. We will take each step in the procedure without unreasonable delay and arrange meetings at reasonable times and locations.
2. Meetings will be conducted in a way that allows both parties to explain their case.
3. Records will be kept detailing the nature of the grievance raised, our response, any action taken and the reasons for it. These records will be kept confidential.
4. You have the right to be accompanied to the hearing by a trade union representative or a co-worker.

16. DBS
Your appointment to this post is subject to an Enhanced check via the Disclosure and Barring Service to confirm you are a suitable person to have substantial access to young people.

17. Confidentiality
You should not divulge **<Name of Organisation>** business to anyone unless expressly authorised to do so.

18. Data Protection/Action against Fraud
You have a duty to ensure that you comply with the rules contained in the Data Protection Act 1984. If you are a data user under the terms of the act, you should ensure that personal data is obtained, held, processed and disclosed legally. Should you require further information concerning this legislation, you should contact your line manager immediately. You should also be aware that payroll information held about you might be used to prevent and detect fraud. The **<Name of Organisation>** Management Committee may also share this information, for the same purposes, with other organisations that handle public funds. Any data generated will be destroyed when enquiries are complete.

19. Health and Safety Regulations, Other Legislations and Club Policies
You are required to familiarise yourself with all relevant regulations, legislation and policies applying to or made by **<Name of Organisation>** Management Committee, and to ensure that you comply with these as required.

20. I acknowledge receipt of my particulars of employment

Signed. ....   Date. ....

Statement of Employment – Shortened Sample

Name of employer: **<Name of Organisation>**
Employer's address: **<Official Address of Management Committee>**

Telephone number: **<Telephone Number of Management Committee>**
Name of employee: **<Employee's Name>**
Job title: **<Job Title>**

1. **Commencement of employment and continuous employment**
   Your employment with **<Name of Organisation>** will begin on **<Start Date>**.

   Your period of continuous employment will begin on **<Start Date>**.

2. **Probation**
   Confirmation of your employment will be subject to the satisfactory completion of a probationary period of **<three/six>** months. During your probationary service, you will be expected to establish your suitability for the job.

3. **Line Management**
   You will be line managed by **<Chairperson of the Management Committee/Staff Member in Charge>**. *{Delete as appropriate; the Staff Member in Charge will be line managed by the Chair, youth workers line managed by the Staff Member in Charge}*

4. **Job description**
   <Enter 'main duties' from job description here>

5. **Job location(s)**
   You will work mainly at the following location:
   <Address of Youth Club>

   Flexibility in terms of location has been agreed.
   You will go on trips and visits with young people when required.

6. **Pay**
   Your rate of pay is £**<XX.XX>** gross per hour. This will be paid monthly in arrears by **<cheque/bank transfer>**. *{Delete as appropriate}*. Your salary will be reviewed on 1 April each year and you will be informed on any rise in salary by 31 April. Any increase will be backdated to 1 April. Annual salary increases are discretionary and not guaranteed.

7. **Hours of work**
   You are employed to work part time.
   Your normal working hours will be **<Number of delivery hours plus portion of management time>** hours per week. *{see below}*
   You will work on the following days: **<Day(s) of the Week>** evening(s).
   You will normally work between the hours of **<Start Time>** and **<Finish Time>**.
   You will occasionally be required to work weekends.

The day(s) of the week you are required to work may change according to the needs of **<Name of Organisation>**. You will be given one month's notice of any change.

Your weekly contracted hours include youth work delivery hours (see normal working hours above) and hours for the following:

- Training: 12 hours per year {*this is the equivalent of two days and is recommended*}
- Supervision: 6 hours per year {*this is one hour every two months and is recommended*}
- Staff Meetings: 6 hours per year {*this two hours each term and is recommended*}

Total management time equals 24 hours per year and your monthly salary includes 2 hours for the above, to be worked in agreement with your manager.

Overtime will not be paid. Working additional hours must be agreed in advance with your line manager and time off in lieu taken.

8. Holidays

You are entitled to 25 days holiday (pro rata) per year.
This excludes public holidays, for which you will receive pro rata paid time off.
Your holiday year begins on 1st April.
Unused entitlement may not be carried forward to the next holiday year.

9. Sickness absence

If you cannot work because of illness, you must inform the Chairperson of the Management Committee as early as possible on the first day and each subsequent day when you are unable to work. Self-certification is allowed for a maximum of 5 days after which a Doctor's Certificate must be provided.

You are entitled to contractual sick pay at your normal rate of pay for a maximum of **<Number of Weeks>** {*recommended 1 week*} (pro rata) for any one period of incapacity. You will be entitled to a maximum of **<Number of Weeks>** {*recommended 4 weeks*} sick pay (pro rata) in any one year. This is subject to the requirements to notify the employer and provide evidence of incapacity. Thereafter, you may be entitled to statutory sick pay.

10. Maternity/Paternity/Adoption Leave

Under the provision of the Employment Rights Act 1996 (as amended by the Employment Act 2002 and regulations there under) eligible employees will be entitled to maternity/paternity/adoption leave.

11. Pension scheme

There is no pension scheme and therefore there is no contracting-out certificate in force for this employment, in England under the Pension Schemes Act 1993, or in Northern Ireland under the Pension Schemes (Northern Ireland) Act 1993.

12. Collective agreements with trade unions

There are no collective agreements with trade unions or other employee groups affecting this employment.

13. Ending the employment

This employment is permanent subject to each party's right to terminate in accordance with the terms of this statement. If you want to leave this employment, you must give **<Number of Weeks>** {*recommended 1 month*} notice. We must give you **<Number of Weeks>** {*recommended 1 month*} notice if we want to end this employment.

14. Disciplinary procedure
This is detailed within the Staff Employment and Management Policy included with this Statement of Employment.

15. Grievance procedure
This is detailed within the Staff Employment and Management Policy included with this Statement of Employment.

16. DBS
Your appointment to this post is subject to an Enhanced check via the Disclosure and Barring Service to confirm that you are a suitable person to have substantial access to young people.

17. Confidentiality
You should not divulge **<Name of Organisation>** business to anyone unless expressly authorised to do so.

18. Data Protection/Action against Fraud
You have a duty to ensure that you comply with the rules contained within the Data Protection Act 1984. Further information is detailed within the Staff Employment and Management Policy included with this Statement of Employment.

19. Health and Safety Regulations, Other Legislations and Club Policies
You are required to familiarise yourself with all relevant regulations, legislation and policies applying to or made by **<Name of Organisation>** Management Committee, and to ensure that you comply with these as required.

20. I acknowledge receipt of my particulars of employment

Signed. ....   Date. ....

DBS Umbrella Organisation Contact Details

Small voluntary youth clubs can access DBS checks through an 'umbrella body'. An umbrella body is a DBS-registered body that allows smaller, non-registered employers to undertake DBS checks. The umbrella body acts as an intermediary between you and the DBS, offering experience that often helps move the process along quickly.

Umbrella bodies in Somerset include:

South Somerset District Council,
Brympton Way, Yeovil, BA20 2HT
Contact Steve Barnes on 01935 462462

Sedgemoor District Council,
Bridgwater House, King Square, Bridgwater, TA6 3AR
Contact Karen Thicker on 01278 435458

Taunton Volunteer Action,
Flook House, Belvedere Road, Taunton, TA1 1BT
01823 284470

Mendip & Sedgemoor Volunteer Centre,
19B Monmouth Street, Bridgwater, TA6 5EQ
01278 457685

Mendip Community Support,
9a Market Place, Shepton Mallet, BA4 5AZ
Contact Rachel Pickford on 01749 346830

Somerset Rural Youth Project,
Unit 2, Suprema Estate, Edington, Bridgwater, TA7 9LF
Contact Howard Marsh on 01278 722100

The Volunteer Network (previously Somerset Youth Volunteering Network),
9 Silver Street, Glastonbury, BA6 8BS
Contact Scott McMillan on 01458 836130

Some umbrella bodies charge an administration fee for processing the application.

If you have questions about DBS checks please contact DBS Customer Services on 0870 90 90 811.

© Somerset Youth and Community Service 2013

Interview Questions Record Sheet – Staff Member in Charge

Post Title: Staff Member in Charge

Candidate Name:

Date & Time:

Panel Member Name:

Question	Guideline response required	Interviewee Response Poor ——▶ Excellent					Comments
		1	2	3	4	5	
1. What experience do you have of providing young people with learning experiences?	• Type of experience • Informal learning • Fun aspect						
2. What do you think are important factors to consider when planning youth club programmes?	• Expressed needs/wants of young people • Awareness of local information • Assessment of young people's needs • Mix of fun and education						
3. How would you ensure that all staff, during your session, work well together as a team?	• Clear preparation briefing at the beginning of the session • Clarity of roles and responsibilities • Effective communication • Awareness of what's going on						

© Somerset Youth and Community Service 2013

Question	Guideline response required	Interviewee Response Poor → Excellent					Comments
		1	2	3	4	5	
4. How would you encourage all young people, regardless of ability, to have a say in the running of their youth club?	• Ask young people what they want • Start small and build ways • Find out blocks and remove • Develop sense of responsibility						
5. How would you ensure that the youth club's sessions were safe for all young people and staff?	• Health and safety checks • Awareness of risk assessments and procedures (i.e. fire) • Effective supervision of club • Staff communication • Use of ground rules and sanctions						
6. What is your experience of supervising staff?	• Giving clear direction to staff • Good organisational skills/managing the paperwork • Listening to staff • Encouraging a team approach						
7. What personal qualities do you have that mean we should pick you?	• Likes young people, experience, patience, enthusiastic						
Does this applicant still remain a firm candidate for this post?	• Yes/No/Undecided						
Post-interview discussions:							
Overall impression	• Standard of dress • Attitude • Enthusiasm						

Question	Guideline response required	Interviewee Response Poor ————▶ Excellent					Comments
		1	2	3	4	5	
Will the applicant fit in with staff group?	• Yes/No/Undecided						
Should applicant be offered post?	• Training • DBS • Medical • References						
SCORES							TOTAL SCORE (out of 45)……….

Interview Questions Record Sheet – Youth Worker

Post Title: Youth Worker

Candidate Name:

Date & Time:

Panel Member Name:

Question	Guideline response required	Interviewee Response Poor ⟶ Excellent					Comments
		1	2	3	4	5	
1. Why do you want this job?	• Enthusiasm • Likes young people • Experience						
2. What experience do you have of working with 13-19 year olds and what skills do you have?	• Check answers against person specification						
3. What do you think are the issues that face young people today?	• List of issues, acknowledgement of differences within young people as a group						
4. What experience do you have of providing young people with learning experiences?	• Type of experience • Informal learning • Fun aspect						

Question	Guideline response required	Interviewee Response Poor → Excellent					Comments
		1	2	3	4	5	
5. How would you encourage all young people, regardless of ability, to take part in activities?	• Find out what young people want • Range of activities • Find out blocks and remove • Be guided by young people						
6. Have you ever had to deal with a young person being aggressive toward you? What did you do?	• Assertive but polite • Appropriate response to the situation • Knows when to ask for assistance from colleagues • Respect						
7. How would you encourage quieter young people to have their say in the running of the club?	• One-to-one chats • Surveys • Start small & build confidence						
8. What personal qualities do you have that mean we should pick you?	• Likes young people, experience, patience, enthusiastic						
9. Does this applicant remain a firm candidate for this post?	• Yes/No/Undecided						
Post Interview discussions:							
Overall impression	Standard of dress, attitude, etc.						
Will the applicant fit in with staff group?	• Yes/No/Undecided						

Question	Guideline response required	Interviewee Response					Comments
		Poor ──→ Excellent					
		1	2	3	4	5	
Should applicant be offered post?	• Training • DBS • Medical • References						
SCORES							TOTAL SCORE (out of 45)…………

Community Youth Club Handbook

Interview Questions Record Sheet – Youth Support Worker

Post Title: Youth Support Worker

Date & Time:

Candidate Name:

Panel Member Name:

Question	Guideline response required	Interviewee Response Poor ——→ Excellent					Comments
		1	2	3	4	5	
1. Why do you want this job?	• Enthusiasm • Likes young people						
2. What experience do you have of working with 13-19 year olds and what skills do you have?	• Check answers against person specification						
3. What do you think is important to young people today?	• List of issues, acknowledgement of difficulties facing young people						
4. How would you encourage all young people, regardless of ability, to take part in activities?	• Find out what young people want • Range of activities • Be guided by young people						

© Somerset Youth and Community Service 2013

Question	Guideline response required	Interviewee Response Poor→Excellent 1	2	3	4	5	Comments
5. Have you ever had to deal with a young person being aggressive toward you? What did you do?	• Assertive but polite • Knows when to ask for assistance from colleagues • Respect						
6. What would you do if a young person asked for your advice?	• Check out information before giving it • Ask for help from staff if needed • Try to help young people come to their own decision, not tell them what to do						
7. What personal qualities do you have that mean we should pick you?	• Likes young people, experience, patience, enthusiastic						
8. Does this applicant remain a firm candidate for this post?	• Yes/No/Undecided						

Post Interview discussions:

Question	Guideline response required	Interviewee Response Poor→Excellent 1	2	3	4	5	Comments
Overall impression	Standard of dress, attitude, etc.						
Will the applicant fit in with staff group?	• Yes/No/Undecided						
Should applicant be offered post?	• Training • DBS • Medical • References						

Question	Guideline response required	Interviewee Response					Comments
		Poor ──→ Excellent					
		1	2	3	4	5	
	SCORES						TOTAL SCORE (out of 45)……….

Appendix 41

Sample Job Description – Staff Member in Charge

Employer: <Name of Organisation>
Job Title: Staff Member in Charge – <Name of Organisation>
Reports To: Chairperson of <Name of Organisation> Management Committee
Base: <Name and Address of Youth Club>

1. Main Purposes of Job

1.1 To have operational responsibility for **<Name of Organisation>** under the guidance of the Chairperson of **<Name of Organisation>** Management Committee and devise and deliver programmes which meet the needs of young people and **<Name of Town/Village>**.

1.2 To be actively involved in face to face youth work with young people aged 11-19 years.

2. Main Responsibilities and Duties

2.1 To build positive relationships and work with young people and staff in **<Name of Organisation>** in order to identify and address young people's interests and needs and address them within available resources.

2.2 To plan, deliver and evaluate youth work programmes and to identify a programme designed to meet the interests and needs of young people.

2.3 To ensure youth work delivery is educative, empowering, participative and fun and reflects equality of opportunity and diversity in all regards. To ensure young people are aware of the positive activities, opportunities and support available to them via partner agencies.

2.4 To keep recordings of the youth work for monitoring and evaluation. Also to ensure that any required data is accurately collected and submitted within the required timescales and also that all administrative requirements are met.

2.5 To attend appropriate management committee and inter-agency meetings if required and provide or contribute to any related reports on the club's work, which reflect the needs and interests of young people and how they are being addressed.

2.6 To assist with the recruitment of staff and to line manage and support paid and voluntary staff. Also to help develop the staff team with the support of the line manager in accordance with Staff Employment and Management Policy.

2.7 To ensure that procedures and practices in the club comply with **<Name of Organisation>** Management Committee policies and legal requirements especially with regard to health and safety, child protection, equality and diversity, and financial regulations. Any concerns should be brought to the attention of the line manager.

2.8 To contribute to the development of youth provision in the area by reflecting young people's needs to relevant agencies.

2.9 To have responsibility for identified resources and budgets and for their efficient and effective use.

© Somerset Youth and Community Service 2013

2.10   To establish supportive and effective working relationships with other professionals providing services for young people in the area. To operate as a team leader with the support of the line manager.

2.11   The post holder may be required to undertake additional duties commensurate with this level of post.

3.   Personal Development

3.1   Regular supervision will take place as reflected in the relevant Staff Employment and Management Policy.

3.2   The contracted hours include a requirement to attend team and other meetings, supervision and training, which will be notified in advance.

4.   Decision Making

The post holder will have delegated powers with respect to the identification of programmes in response to young people's needs, and to operational aspects of the club. Any matters of concern/development should be discussed and agreed with the line manager.

5.   Contacts and Relationships

The post holder will:

Work with: Young people aged 11-19
              Colleagues in other organisations providing services to young people
              Management committee and the local community
              Schools/colleges

Liaise with: Appropriate statutory and voluntary organisations

Be a member of: **<Name of Organisation>** staff team
                    Other groups as appropriate

6.   Problem Solving and Creativity

6.1   The post requires a creative approach to the development and delivery of youth work in a way that involves young people themselves. A flexible approach is required.

6.2   Strategic leadership will be offered by the Chairperson of the **<Name of Organisation>** Management Committee.

7.   Additional Information

7.1   The post holder is required to work evenings and weekends and at times may be involved in residential work (with due notice).

7.2   May be required to travel across an area where public transport is not easily available, particularly out of business hours.

© Somerset Youth and Community Service 2013

Terms and Conditions

1.   The post will be paid pro rata **<Annual Yearly Salary>**.

2.   The post requires an enhanced Disclosure and Barring Service (DBS) check and satisfactory completion of a **<three/six>** month probationary period.

3.   The work will involve evening and weekend commitments.

4.   The annual leave entitlement is pro rata 25 days plus bank holidays, to be taken at times agreed with the line manager.

5.   The appointment will be terminable on either side by giving **<X>** months' notice.

6.   An appropriate travel allowance will be paid.

228

PERSON SPECIFICATION

Post Title: Staff Member in Charge of **<Name of Organisation>**
Salary: **<Hourly rate and equivalent full-time salary>**

Key Competencies

- Knowledge and experience of youth work – preferably in a range of settings
- Ability to communicate with a wide range of young people and adults
- Have effective interpersonal skills

Able to:
- Establish and maintain positive relationships with young people
- Encourage participation by young people
- Empower them through an educational process
- Address equality and diversity issues
- Identify, plan, develop and deliver programmes that respond to young people's needs
- Create a positive environment for work with young people
- Give guidance and leadership to staff

2. Qualifications

Essential	Desirable
NVQ/VRQ Level 3 Qualification in Youth & Community Work as recognized by the JNC for Youth and Community Workers; or a commitment to achieving a relevant Level 3 qualification within 2 years of appointment.	<ul><li>First aid training</li><li>Other qualifications relevant to work with young people/management of staff and resources</li><li>Other relevant qualifications</li><li>Clean driving licence</li><li>Qualification in specialist curriculum area e.g. outdoor education, arts, health, ICT</li><li>Staff supervision</li><li>Health and safety training</li></ul>

3. Work experience

Essential	Desirable
<ul><li>Face to face youth work with young people aged 11-19 that demonstrates the ability to establish positive and productive relationships with them</li><li>Programme planning and curriculum development</li><li>Monitoring and evaluation of youth work</li><li>Support of young people's participation</li><li>Work within a team</li><li>Group work skills</li></ul>	<ul><li>1 year as a NVQ/VRQ Level 3 qualified youth worker</li><li>Youth work experience in a range of settings</li><li>Financial knowledge and administration</li><li>Work with management committees and local communities</li><li>Team or project or club leadership and development</li><li>Supervision/line management of paid or voluntary staff</li><li>Inter-agency work</li><li>Equalities and diversity implementation Risk management</li></ul>

© Somerset Youth and Community Service 2013

Knowledge

Essential	Desirable
• Awareness of contemporary youth issues and influences • Curriculum development and programme planning • Health & safety implementation as it relates to youth work • Monitoring and evaluation of youth work • Equalities and diversity in practice • Ability to interpret and apply guidelines and documentation relevant to youth work with young people	• Child protection • Administrative systems • Risk management • Resources and building management functions • ICT use for administration and curriculum delivery • Policies related to work with young people • Report writing • Agencies working with young people • Supervision of staff • Research skills • Resources and premises management • Able to prepare club plan

Personal Qualities

Essential	Desirable
• Minimum age 18 years • Self-motivation and also ability to motivate young people and adults. • Able to work independently • Team leadership and membership • Flexible approach • Able to work evenings (and occasional weekends) • Integrity, honesty and discretion • Positive attitude to young people and empathy with and interest in their development • Commitment to personal development • Demonstration of a commitment to safeguarding and promoting the welfare of children and young people	• Creative approach • Systematic in approach • Confident approach

Sample Job Description – Youth Worker

Employer: <Name of Organisation>
Job Title: Youth Worker
Reports To: Staff Member in Charge
Base: <Name and Address of Youth Club>

1. Main Purposes of Job

1.2 To be actively involved in face to face youth work with young people aged 11-19 years in a way that meets the needs of young people and **<Name of Town/Village>**.

1.3 To identify the needs and interests of young people and devise or contribute to appropriate programmes and curriculum to meet them.

2. Main Responsibilities and Duties

2.1 To work with young people and staff in the club in order to establish positive relationships; to identify and address young people's interests and needs within available resources.

2.2 To contribute to the planning, delivery and evaluation of programmes designed to meet the interests and needs of young people. This is to be done in a way that encourages and supports them to take a full and active part in the decision making processes involved.

2.3 To make an effective contribution to the capacity of the club to deliver youth work, which is educative, empowering, participative and fun and which also reflects equality of opportunity and diversity in all regards. Also to make young people aware of the positive activities and opportunities and support available to them via partner agencies.

2.4 To keep the required youth work and other recordings and carry out monitoring and evaluation of the youth work taking place as required.

2.5 To establish supportive and effective working relationships with other staff and work as an effective team member within the club.

2.6 To lead or take joint responsibility for youth work delivery, if required. To give associated direction to staff and volunteers as part of this delivery session if required.

2.7 In fulfilling the main tasks, to adhere to the procedures and policies as required in order to comply with **<Name of Organisation>** Management Committee policies and legal requirements e.g. health and safety, child protection safeguarding, equality and diversity, and financial regulations. Any concerns should to be brought to the attention of the relevant line manager.

2.8 To contribute to the development of relationships with community groups and other agencies if required.

2.9 To contribute to the collation of management information and administrative requirements under the guidance of a line manager.

© Somerset Youth and Community Service 2013

2.10 The post holder may be required to undertake additional duties commensurate with this level of post.

3. **Personal Development**

3.1 Regular supervision will take place as reflected in the **\<Name of Organisation\>** Staff Employment and Management Policy.

3.2 The contracted hours include a requirement to attend team and other meetings, supervision and training, which will be notified in advance.

4. **Decision Making**

The post holder will have delegated powers with respect to operational aspects of the club when acting as Staff Member in Charge. Any matters of concern/development should be discussed and agreed with the line manager.

5. **Contacts and Relationships**

The post holder will:

Work with: Young people aged 11-19 years
Other agencies/organisations as appropriate
Management committee and the local community

Liaise with: Appropriate statutory and voluntary organisations

Be a member of: **\<Name of Organisation\>** staff team
Other groups as appropriate

6. **Problem Solving and Creativity**

6.1 The post holder will primarily carry out the tasks outlined under the direction of a line manager. The post requires a creative approach to the development and delivery of youth work in the club in a way that involves young people themselves. A flexible approach is required.

6.2 Line management will be given by the Staff Member in Charge of **\<Name of Organisation\>**.

7. **Additional Information**

7.1 The post holder is required to work evenings and weekends and at times may be asked to be involved in residential work (with due notice).

7.2 The post holder may be required to travel across an area where public transport is not easily available, particularly out of business hours.

Terms and Conditions

1. The post will be paid pro rata **\<Annual Yearly Salary\>**.
2. The post requires an enhanced criminal background check and satisfactory completion of a **\<three/six\>** month probationary period.
3. The work will involve evening and weekend commitments.
4. The annual leave entitlement is pro rata 25 days plus bank holidays, to be taken at times agreed with the line manager.
5. The appointment will be terminable on either side by giving 3 months' notice.
6. An appropriate travel allowance will be paid.

© Somerset Youth and Community Service 2013

PERSON SPECIFICATION

Post Title: Youth Worker **\<Name of Organisation\>**

Salary: **\<Hourly Rate and Equivalent Full-Time Salary\>**

1. Key Competencies

- Knowledge and experience of youth work
- Ability to communicate with a wide range of young people and adults
- Demonstrate effective interpersonal skills

Able to:
- Establish and maintain positive relationships with young people
- Encourage participation by young people
- Identify and respond to young people's interests and needs
- Plan and deliver programmes
- Contribute to the creation of a positive environment for work with young people

2. Qualifications

Essential	Desirable
NVQ/VRQ Level 3 Qualification in Youth & Community Work as recognised by the JNC for Youth and Community Workers	<ul><li>First aid training</li><li>Other qualifications relevant to work with young people/management of staff and resources</li><li>Qualification in specialist curriculum area e.g. outdoor education, arts, health, ICT</li></ul>

3. Work experience

Essential	Desirable
<ul><li>Face to face youth work with young people aged 13-19 which reflects the ability to establish positive and productive relationships with them</li><li>Programme planning and delivery</li><li>Work within a team</li><li>Group work skills</li></ul>	<ul><li>1 year as a NVQ/VRQ Level 3 qualified youth worker</li><li>Experience of adolescent young people in a range of youth work settings</li><li>Financial knowledge/administration</li><li>Work with local communities</li><li>Young people's participation/empowerment</li></ul>

233

4. Knowledge	
Essential	**Desirable**
• Awareness of contemporary youth issues and influences • Curriculum development and programme planning • Health & safety awareness/knowledge in respect of work with young people • Ability to interpret and apply guidelines and documentation relevant to youth work with young people • Understanding the nature of, and able to, contribute to the positive development of a positive environment for working with young people • Equalities and diversity in practice	• Knowledge and expertise in identified curriculum area e.g. outdoor education, health • Monitoring and evaluation of youth work • ICT use for administration and curriculum delivery • Report writing • Resources management

Personal Qualities	
Essential	**Desirable**
• Minimum age 18 years • Positive attitude to young people and empathy with and interest in their development • Self-motivation and also ability to motivate young people and adults • Can take responsibility and can work autonomously if required • Ability to work as part of a team • Flexible – able to work evenings (and occasional weekends) • Integrity, honesty and discretion • Commitment to personal development • Demonstration of a commitment to safeguarding and promoting the welfare of children and young people	• Creative approach • Systematic in approach • Confident approach

Sample Job Description – Youth Support Worker

Employer: <Name of Organisation>
Job Title: Youth Support Worker
Reports To: Staff Member in Charge
Base: <Name and Address of Youth Club>

1. Main Purposes of Job

1.1 To establish positive working relationships and work with young people aged 11-19 years in a way that meets the needs of young people and the requirements of **<Name of Town/Village>**.

2. Main Responsibilities and Duties

2.1 Under the direction of the line manager to be actively involved in direct youth work with young people in a way that includes a commitment to young people's participation.

2.2 To contribute to the planning, delivery and evaluation of programmes designed to meet the interests and needs of young people in **<Name of Organisation>** under the direction of the line manager.

2.3 To contribute to the planning, monitoring and evaluation of youth work taking place as part of the youth work team.

2.4 To establish supportive and effective working relationships with youth work staff and to work within a team as an effective team member. To contribute to the development of a positive environment for work with young people.

2.5 To ensure, under the direction of the line manager, that in fulfilling the main tasks, the procedures and policies adopted comply with **<Name of Organisation>** Management Committee policies and legal requirements especially health and safety, child protection, equality and diversity, and financial regulations. Any concerns are to be brought to the attention of the line manager.

2.6 To contribute to day to day administration in order to ensure the smooth running of the youth club.

2.7 The post holder may be required to undertake additional duties commensurate with this level of post.

3. Personal Development

3.1 Regular supervision will take place as reflected in the **<Name of Organisation>** Staff Employment and Management Policy.

3.2 The contracted hours include the requirement to attend team and other meetings, supervision and training, which will be notified in advance.

4. **Decision Making**

This post is largely about gaining the experience of working and interacting with young people.

5. **Contacts and Relationships**

The post holder will:

Work with: Young people in the 11-19 years priority age range
             Other agencies/organisations as appropriate
             Schools

Liase with: Appropriate statutory and voluntary organisations

Be a member of: **<Name of Organisation>** staff team
                  Other groups as appropriate

6. **Problem Solving**

6.1   The post holder will carry out the tasks outlined under the direction and supervision of a line manager. Initiative and independent action will be limited as staff appointed will undertake duties under direction.

6.2   Line management will be given by the Staff Member in Charge of **<Name of Organisation>**.

7. **Additional Information**

7.1   The post holder is required to work evenings and weekends and at times may be asked to be involved in residential work (with due notice).

7.2   The post holder may be required to travel across an area where public transport is not easily available, particularly out of business hours.

Terms and Conditions

1.   The post will be paid pro rata **<Annual Yearly Salary>**.
2.   The post requires an enhanced Disclosure and Barring Service (DBS) check and satisfactory completion of a **<three/six>** month probationary period.
3.   The work will involve evening and weekend commitments.
4.   The annual leave entitlement is pro rata 25 days plus bank holidays, to be taken at times agreed with the line manager.
5.   The appointment will be terminable on either side by giving 3 months' notice.
6.   An appropriate travel allowance will be paid.

PERSON SPECIFICATION

Post Title: Youth Support Worker **<Name of Organisation>**

Salary: **<Hourly Rate and Equivalent Full-Time Salary>**

1.	**Key Competencies**

- Able to communicate with a wide range of young people and adults
- Able to empathise with and take an interest in young people's development
- Able to be a team player
- Able to contribute to the creation of a positive working environment for work with young people

2.	**Qualifications**

Essential	Desirable
	• NVQ/VRQ Level 2 qualification in youth and community work as recognised by the JNC (Youth & Community Work) • Qualifications related to work with young people e.g. counselling, group work, specialist activities (such as the arts, outdoor education, ICT etc.) • First aid training • Clean driving licence

3.	**Work Experience**

Essential	Desirable
	• Experience of adolescent young people • Youth work delivery in the voluntary or statutory sector • Programme planning and delivery • Financial knowledge/administration systems • Experience of working with a range of adults

Knowledge	

Essential	Desirable
• Ability to interpret and apply guidelines and documentation relevant to work with young people • Ability to contribute to the creation of a positive environment for working with young people	• Health and safety in respect of youth work programme and activities delivery including child protection • Contemporary youth issues • Programme planning • Equalities and diversity in practice • Organisational skills • Effective listening skills

Personal Qualities	
Essential	**Desirable**
• Effective interpersonal skills • Positive attitude towards young people • Flexible – able to work evenings (and weekends on occasions) • Empathises with and takes an interest in young people's development • Willing to develop skills and take advantage of training available • Integrity, honesty and discretion • Minimum age 18 years • Able to work as a member of a team	• Creative approach • Willingness to participate in residential work if required

Volunteer Memorandum of Understanding Sample

1. Parties to the agreement

Employer: Volunteer:
<Name and Address>   **<Name and Address>**

2. <Name of Organisation>, <Job Title> and <Date of Employment>

You are employed as **<Job Title>**.
Your employment in this role will commence on **<Start Date>**.
You are employed to work in **<Name of Organisation>**, at **<Address>**. Your line manager will be **<Name of Line Manager>**.
Your main tasks will be **<Insert Detail from Job Description>**

-
-
-

The **<Name of Organisation>** Management Committee undertakes to provide adequate information, training and support to the volunteer.
The volunteer undertakes to abide by **<Name of Organisation>** Management Committee policies and procedures when carrying out tasks relating to the volunteer role.

3. Working Arrangements

Your working hours will be **<Times>** on **<Days>**.
You are required, as appropriate, to take part in staff meetings and to attend supervision meetings with your line manager.

4. Notice
Both parties are required to give 2 weeks' notice of their intention to terminate this agreement. This notice should be provided in writing.

5. Health and Safety
The **<Name of Organisation>** Management Committee places great emphasis on the health, safety and welfare of its volunteers, paid staff and young people. The **<Name of Organisation>** Management Committee health, safety and welfare policy is available at your place of work; you are recommended to familiarise yourself with this document. Please speak to your line manager if you require further information.

6. Confidentiality
You should not divulge confidential **<Name of Organisation>** Management Committee information to anyone unless expressly authorised to do so.

7. DBS

Your appointment is subject to the completion of an Enhanced Disclosure via the Disclosure and Barring Service.

8. Signatures

On behalf of the **<Name of Organisation>** Management Committee:

Name:
Signature:

Position:
Date:

Volunteer
Name:

Signature:

Date:

I acknowledge receipt of this agreement and I understand and will abide by its contents.

Roles & Responsibility Sample Sheet

Youth Club Name:	Kittsville Youth Club				
Programme Dates:	March & April 2011				

Date & Staff working	Session programme item	Staff responsible for preparation	Resources needed	Staff delivering item	Notes
14/03/11 Lilith Chloe Barry Pandora	Team Games	Chloe	Games sheet Bats & balls Old clothes Cutlery and knife Hula hoops	Chloe	Chloe to check risk assessment. Charity shop has clean clothes if we can't find any – but must return them clean! Get chocolate from tuck shop.
	Pizza making	Barry	Pizza bases, toppings and a sharp knife	Barry	Budget of £10 – Barry will get money back from treasurer – don't forget the receipts.
	Smoking quiz	Pandora	Quiz from internet	Lilith	Pandora will copy quiz at work.
21/03/11 Lilith Malachi Hengist Jasmine	Programme planning	Lilith	Paper, pens and biscuits	Lilith	Do this after the dance session so everyone can get involved.
	Dance session	Malachi	70's CD and player	Malachi & Mrs Dixon	Malachi to check Mrs Dixon is still coming.
	Food bingo	Hengist	Selection of non-British food from deli, blindfolds	Hengist	Budget of £8, Hengist will reclaim money.

Supervision Record Sample

Post Holder:	
Line Manager:	
Meeting Date:	

Agenda
1.
2.
3.
4.
5.
6.
7.
8.

Agenda Item:	Action by:

Agenda Item:	Action by:

Signed:		
		Line manager
Date:		
Signed:		
		Staff member
Date:		

Suppliers of Payroll Services

Payroll and personnel support for voluntary sector and community groups

Management committees running their own youth club have a variety of options when employing their own paid staff.

Larger committees may have the capacity to run their own payroll and deal with tax and personnel issues. Smaller committees that don't have the capacity to deal with payroll and HR issues, but can afford to employ paid staff, can access support through organisations that offer personnel and payroll bureau services. The following offer this service in Somerset specifically for voluntary groups:

Taunton Volunteer Action
TVA offers DBS processing and payroll bureau services. TVA provides payslips and P60s and completes the annual filing with HMRC. The voluntary organisation is responsible for paying its staff based on the information provided by TVA. This service is accessible to TVA members across Somerset.
Call 01823 284470 for more information.

Community Accounting and Bookkeeping Service (a subsidiary of Vista Project)
CAaBS offers a comprehensive payroll service, which includes end of year returns and electronic filing with HMRC as well as processing monthly payments. In addition, CAaBS provides a wide range of financial and administrative support packages, and their website includes HR advice and information.
For more information or to discuss options, call 08453 580372 or browse www.caabs.org.uk.

South Somerset Voluntary and Community Action
SSVCA provides a full payroll service (includes holiday, P45s and P60s) for voluntary and independent organisations.
Contact SSVCA on 01935 475914.

Somerset Rural Youth Project
SRYP can provide a professional staff recruitment, management and payroll service as part of its youth club support programme. There are a variety of options, depending on the size of the club, number of staff and contract size.
For more information or to discuss the various options, contact SRYP on 01278 722100.

Payroll, accountancy and other financial services are also available from a range of commercial providers. These are generally aimed at small and medium-sized businesses rather than voluntary groups, but may offer cost-effective packages.

This information is provided in good faith and no recommendation for any service or provider is intended or should be inferred.

Service Specification Sample

Town/Village/Area youth club/project
2012/13

Project specification and invitation to tender

1   Project Aim

1.1   The **<XXX Town/Village/Area> <Youth Club/Project>** will provide young people aged 11-19 from **<XXX>** with support to develop and improve their personal and social skills using an open access youth work approach.

1.2   The **<XXX Town/Parish Council/Committee>** will use a non-prescriptive, flexible commissioning approach to encourage providers to submit proposals for innovative provision.

2   Context

2.1   Something about the size and shape of the area/town/village, notable features, number of 11-19 years olds, etc.

2.2   Any specific issues that should be addressed by the project (anti-social behaviour, health issues, crime, etc.) should be noted here, but not the solution or the targeted reduction in the incidence of the issue.

3   Project objectives

3.1   The youth club/project will be expected to:

    3.1.1   Provide a universally-accessible year-round service

    3.1.2   Provide social and personal development opportunities for young people aged 11-19 which add value to formal education and their other experiences

    3.1.3   Involve young people in the planning and delivery of the project

    3.1.4   Deliver effective and innovative services

    3.1.5   Maintain appropriate records and report on young people's outcomes, progress and development

    3.1.6   Recruit, train and support a team of up to **<XX>** volunteers

    3.1.7   Run a coffee bar within the provision offering healthy snacks and drinks

    3.1.8   Add extras, delete any that aren't relevant

4   Key performance indicators

4.1   The project's minimum success output indicators are:

Output	Indicator	Comments
Delivery sessions	47 weeks across the year	
Opening hours	2 hours per week, from 7pm	Thursday evening

Average attendance	25 per session	Average over three months
Age profile	At least 50% aged 14+	
Gender profile	Between 60/40 and 40/60 M/F	
Written report	Termly	To parish/town council
Young people's origin	Minimum 80% from XX area	
Plus others as appropriate		

4.2   The project's outcome indicators include:

Outcome	Indicator	Comments
Reduction in anti-social behaviour	Number of calls about young people	Data termly from police
Young people are actively involved in community activity	Volunteering hours V-inspired certificates D of E participation	Termly presentation
Young people enjoy and value the provision	% of young people expressing satisfaction with service	Six-monthly survey
Young people's achievements are recognised	Accredited awards achieved – Endeavour Credit; DofE; Asdan; etc.	Termly presentation
Community members support the provision	Number of adult volunteers engaged £ raised locally	
And others…		
And yet more…		

5   Resources

5.1   The maximum value of the contract is £xxx for the 2012/13 financial year.

5.2   In addition to the contract value, the provider can generate income to support the project through charging subscriptions at a maximum of **<XX>**p per person per session and the provision of a coffee bar serving healthy snacks and drinks.

5.3   Charges for other activities must be reasonable and a full budget breakdown must be available for inspection by the council/committee on request.

5.4   The youth club building at **<XXX Street>** is available for the project's delivery. Running and reasonable maintenance and repair costs for the building will be met by the town/parish council/committee. Any unexpected damage must be reported to the council/committee and where the provider is deemed negligent the cost of repairs may be reclaimed.

6 Indemnities

6.1 The provider is expected to confirm in writing that all relevant requirements under legislation and good practice are met, but especially in relation to:

Safeguarding and child protection	Health and safety	Financial monitoring
Food safety and hygiene	Parental consent	Data protection
Employment of staff	Organisational experienc	Governance

6.2 The provider is expected to maintain a minimum of £5m public liability insurance for the duration of the contract to cover service users, members of the public and the premises used for delivery.

6.3 **<XX Town/Parish Council/Committee>** shall be indemnified from liability for acts or omissions by the provider for the duration of the contracted delivery.

7 Timing and deadlines

7.1 The timescale for awarding the contract is:

Application process opens	On publication of this document
Open event for potential providers to meet the council/committee and young people, and to discu the project	**<Thursday XX March>**
Deadline for competed tenders to be received	**<Friday XX March>**
Provider interviews (if required)	A week later
Contract awarded and all applicants notified	A week later
Contract start	As soon as possible

8 Structure of proposals

8.1 Tenders should include:

- A description of the proposed work
- Where appropriate, a detailed work plan including key dates, milestones and deliverables
- A summary of relevant organisational experience
- CVs of key personnel proposed for this project, including relevant experience and qualifications
- An assessment of the risks associated with the project and how these will be managed
- A budget profile showing costs associated with staff, management, training, resources etc.

8.2 Tendering organisations should clearly demonstrate:

- Knowledge and understanding of the area and related issues
- Experience of undertaking similar work
- An understanding of the outputs, outcomes and deliverables

© Somerset Youth and Community Service 2013

- An appropriate mix of skills for the project, including rationale for collaboration in the case of consortia bids for this project
- The risks associated with the project have been considered
- Clear, easy to understand costs for the project, with a clear rationale provided

9   Terms and conditions

9.1   Cost of tenders: Tendering organisations will not be reimbursed for any expenses incurred in the preparation and submission of a tender.

9.2   Right to reject tenders: The council/committee is not bound to accept the lowest or any tender.

9.3   Acceptance of a tender: No tender shall be deemed to be accepted until acceptance has been notified in writing by the council/committee.

9.4   Validity period: Your tender should remain open for acceptance for a period of 90 days from the deadline for the receipt of tenders.

9.5   The provider shall not, without the written consent of the council/committee, transfer or assign the benefit of any order or sub-let any portion thereof.

9.6   Nothing herein contained shall prevent the council/committee purchasing any service or provision of the type that is the subject of the tender from any other source whether a tenderer or not.

9.7   In the event of:

i)   the provider's failure to execute the contract within the stipulated time scales; or

ii)   the provider failing to fulfil any condition in the contract or request (in respect of which the council/committee's authorised officer shall be the sole judge); or

iii)   the provider becoming bankrupt or insolvent or entering into liquidation or in the event of an Administration Order or arrangement with his creditors.

The council/committee shall have full immediate power to cancel the contract without charge and to commission the service from any other person or body, and may deduct any extra costs associated with the contract cancellation from sums due to the provider.

9.8   The provider shall exercise all reasonable skill, care and diligence in the discharge and the provision of the service and will only employ such persons who have adequate knowledge and are competent to provide such services.

9.9   The sum payable to the successful tenderer by the council/committee under this contract shall constitute the only remuneration in connection with the service.

9.10   The provider will be paid quarterly in arrears subject to the successful completion of monitoring processes as agreed.

This specification was agreed by
<XXX Town/Parish Council/Committee>
on **<XX March 2013>**.

Time Record Sample

Name:

Date	Hours worked	Activity

Building Booking Form Sample

Booking form for <Name of Organisation>

This form must be completed in full and returned to the
address below at least 14 days before the proposed booking.

Hirer	
Name of group or organisation:	
Contact person:	
Contact address:	
Invoice address (if different):	
Telephone:	Email:

I have been provided with a copy and agree to the conditions of hire, which apply to this booking. I agree to the cost of the booking and will ensure payment is made.

Signed:		Date:

Booking details			
Date(s):			
Areas required: (please circle)	<Social area	Meeting room	Kitchen>
Time:	From:	To:	
	(Please include enough setting up and clearing away time)		
Purpose of booking:			
Number of attendees:			
Refreshments: (£1.50 per person)	Tea & coffee	Squash	Biscuits	Etc.
Insurance: (please tick)	Own cover in place (please enclose certificate)	<Name of Organisation> cover required (12.5% surcharge)	

For office use			
Form received:		Deposit rec'd or invoice sent:	
Booking confirmed (Y/N):		By:	
Final payment rec'd:			

Please return the completed form to **<Name, Address and Email of Organisation>**.
Cheques should be payable to **<Name of Bank Account>**.

Building Conditions of Hire Sample

Conditions of Hire for <Name of Building>

1. APPLICATION FOR HIRE

1.1 Applications for hire of **<Name of Building>** must be made on the official booking form. Applications should be received at least 14 days prior to the hire period.

1.2 Receipt of a booking form does not constitute an acceptance of the hire by **<Name of Organisation>**. The premises shall not be deemed to be booked until the applicant has received confirmation in writing from **<Name of Organisation>**.

1.3 All applicants must be over the age of 21 and proof of identity/age may be required.

1.4 All bookings are subject to the dates and times stated on the booking form. Hirers must ensure that the building is vacated at the appropriate time. Entry to the building will be from the time specified on the booking form. Additional time will be charged after the event, if necessary.

1.5 All groups and organisations using the premises must state the purpose for which they are engaged and shall not sublet or alter the purpose for which they are engaged without the consent of **<Name of Organisation>**. If the building, or any part thereof, is used for purposes different from that for which they are engaged, **<Name of Organisation>** reserves the right to terminate the booking at any time without **<Name of Organisation>** being liable to the hirer for costs incurred by the group or organisation.

1.6 All applications must state the specific areas of accommodation within the facility required. No other areas of the facility, apart from the toilets and foyer as a means of access, will be available as part of the hire.

1.7 **The use of the premises must not interfere with the proper working of the establishment or impair its efficiency. In particular, the hirer acknowledges that it will not have exclusive use of the site.**

1.8 No application for hire will be accepted while any accounts for payment by the hirer to **<Name of Organisation>** remain outstanding.

1.9 **<Name of Organisation>** reserves the right to grant or refuse any booking application in whole or in part without giving any reason.

2. ADVANCE BOOKING

2.1 Bookings can be made up to one year in advance of the required date.

2.2 Advance applications for bookings of a continual or repetitive nature are accepted at the discretion of **<Name of Organisation>**.

3. PAYMENT

3.1 Payment is required at least 7 days in advance of the booking for one-off hire periods.

3.2   **<Name of Organisation>** reserves the right to levy additional charges as a result of any damage, after the hire period.

3.3   No booking will be accepted where the hirer has outstanding charges for previous hires.

4.   CANCELLATION

4.1   **<Name of Organisation>** reserves the right to cancel a booking without being liable for compensation in the event of facilities being required for purposes deemed necessary by **<Name of Organisation>**.

4.2   Notification of the hirer's intention to cancel a booking must be made in writing. In the event of cancellation by the hirer the following charges are payable:

    a.   More than 14 days – No charge
    b.   7 to 14 days in advance – 50% of hire charge
    c.   Less than 7 days in advance – 100% of hire charge

5.   LOSS, INJURY OR DAMAGE

5.1   The hirer is responsible for any loss or damage to the building, fixtures, fittings, contents and décor during the hire period.

5.2   The hirer is advised that **<Name of Organisation>** cannot accept responsibility in respect of loss or theft of articles from the premises during the hire period or any articles left on the premises at any time.

5.3   **<Name of Organisation>** accepts no responsibility for any loss or damage, including personal injury and death, resulting from the premises proving to be unsuitable for the hirer's intended use.

5.4   The hirer is advised to take out appropriate insurance to cover loss or damage of property belonging to themselves, **<Name of Organisation>** or members of the public and to cover death or injury of persons in the building during the period of hire.

5.5   When an event is open to the public, the hirer is required to ensure sufficient public liability insurance and the premises are hired on the understanding that this will be done. Evidence of insurance cover must be provided before the booking will be confirmed. No evidence will result in the booking not being accepted.

5.6   The hirer must indemnify **<Name of Organisation>** against any loss or damage as described within these conditions.

6.   LAYOUT & CAPACITY

6.1   The hirer must adhere to the agreed capacities for the spaces booked. Failure to comply with the capacities may result in the termination of the hire at any time without **<Name of Organisation>** being liable to the hirer for damages.

6.2   Car parking at the premises is strictly limited and hirers should not expect parking to be available. Arrangements for parking must be discussed and agreed at the time of booking.

252

7. HEALTH AND SAFETY

7.1 Any portable electrical appliance not provided by **<Name of Organisation>** must have a valid portable appliance test label or certificate. If the valid label or certificate is not available this equipment must not be used in the premises.

7.2 The hirer must ensure all gangways, doorways, stairways, exits, emergency exits and entrances are kept unobstructed at all times.

7.3 Hirers must make themselves aware of fire regulations and procedures in force and as outlined in the fire evacuation notices displayed in the building.

7.4 Hirers should ensure they have at least one person who is trained in fire safety on the premises at all times during the hire period.

7.5 No explosives, highly flammable spirits or liquid gas containers shall be brought into the premises and the use of naked lights in any part of the building is prohibited.

7.6 All chemicals and hazardous substances must be transported, stored and used in accordance with COSHH regulations. The proposed use of chemicals or hazardous substances must be included in the booking form.

7.7 Any accident must be reported as soon as possible to **<Name of Responsible Person, Address and Telephone Number, Name of Organisation>**.

8. PROPERTY AND EQUIPMENT

8.1 Property brought into the building by hirers must be removed at the end of the hire period unless otherwise authorised by **<Name of Organisation>**. Failure to remove equipment will result in charges to cover temporary removal and storage of the items involved.

8.2 Hirers should not interfere with electrical fixtures and fittings. No extension from existing electrical fittings shall be made without the consent of **<Name of Organisation>**.

8.3 No fittings of any kind (bolt, nails, screws, BluTack etc.) shall be attached to any part of the interior or exterior of the building without prior consent from **<Name of Organisation>**.

8.4 Hirers must leave the premises in a clean and tidy condition. Failure to do so will result in additional charges to cover cleaning.

9. NOTICE AND DISPLAY BOARDS

9.1 The use of community facility notice and display boards is prohibited unless by prior arrangement with **<Name of Organisation>**.

9.2 No posters, boards, placards, logos, fittings, banners, signs or advertisements or other display materials shall be affixed to any internal or external doors, walls and windows without prior consent from **<Name of Organisation>**.

10. SMOKING

10.1 **<Name of Organisation>** operates a **no smoking** policy in all facilities.

11. SUPPLY OF FOOD AND DRINK

11.1 Food handlers must hold relevant qualifications under the Food Safety Act 1990. Hirers must observe the hygiene guidelines displayed in the kitchen.

11.2 All foodstuffs stored in the kitchen should be labelled to indicate the user and the date of opening. All out of date, perished items will be destroyed.

11.3 No intoxicating liquors (alcohol) are permitted to be bought or sold on the premises.

12. AMENDMENTS TO CONDITIONS

12.1 **<Name of Organisation>** reserves the right to amend or add to these conditions of hire at any time.

13. GENERAL

13.1 For the purpose of these conditions the term '**<Name of Organisation>**' shall include persons authorised by them; the term 'hirer' shall include their employees, agents, tradesmen, contractors, suppliers and members of the general public entering at the invitation, express or implied, of the hirer or their agents, tradesmen, contractors and suppliers.

13.2 **<Name of Organisation>** officers shall have access to all parts of the community facilities at all times during hire periods.

13.3 Advice and instructions of **<Name of Organisation>** must be strictly adhered to at all times during the hire period.

13.4 **<Name of Organisation>** or persons authorised by **<Name of Organisation>** shall have the right to suspend or take action at their discretion on any matter which, in the opinion of the organisation's officers, does not comply with the terms of these conditions, or which they consider necessary in the interests of safety and good order or to deal with any contingency not covered by these Conditions of Hire.

Useful information for groups using your building

Health and Safety and Emergency Procedures

Locations of useful things

Location of telephones:	
Location of incident/accident book:	
Location of first aid kit:	
Location of building risk assessment:	
Location of health and safety file:	

It can be useful for user groups for you to draw the layout of your building and mark the following locations on it:		
• fire escapes • fire extinguishers • fire alarm call points	• fire doors • telephones • first aid kit	• main services switches (electricity, gas, water, etc.) • accessibility (ramps, wide doors etc.)
<It does not have to be to scale – approximate will do.>		

Contact numbers

It can also be useful for user groups to have call out numbers in case of accidents and emergencies. You may wish to only include numbers for the management committee, as you want to contact contractors yourself. However, if user groups can't contact you, if might be useful for them to be able to contact your preferred contractors directly. It's up to you!

	Name	Address	Telephone
Management Committee – Building problems			
Management Committee – Treasurer			
Management Committee – Bookings			
Emergency Repairs			
Alarm System			
Electricity			
Gas			
Water			

You may wish to include the name, addresses and telephone numbers of all the key holders and user groups for your building (ensure you check that they are happy to be included):

It is also useful to include numbers of local emergency services:			
Emergency Services	**Name**	**Address**	**Telephone**
Local Police			
Local Doctor			
Local Hospital			
Casualty Unit			

It is also useful if user groups know who else is using the building and at what time. You can use the table below to record the information.

	Morning	Afternoon	Evening
Monday			
Tuesday			
Wednesday			
Thursday			
Friday			
Saturday			
Sunday			

Ages 13 - 16

Mondays 7:00pm to 9:30pm
@ the Village Hall on the rec

For more information:
Contact Lilith Brown on
01900 000000
www.kittsvilleyouth.co.uk

Confidentiality Notice Sample

Confidentiality

We listen, but we won't tell

If you talk to us, we won't tell anyone about what you've said

The only reason we might have to consider passing on any information that you give us without your permission, would be to protect you or someone else from serious harm. We would always try to talk to you about this first.

If you want to know more about confidentiality, please talk to a member of staff.

Managing Behaviour Guide

Preparation – Young People

→ **Set clear ground rules**
- Ground rules should be few and easily understood.
- Ground rules should preferably describe what a young person should do, not what they shouldn't.
- Ground rules should be clearly displayed.
- Ground rules should be negotiated with the young people if possible.

→ **Set clear consequences for breaking ground rules**
- Consequences should be simple to understand and logical.
- Consequences should be deliverable.
- Consequences should also be negotiated with the young people if possible.

→ **Ensure consequences are staggered and appropriate**
- Consider using a traffic light system (two warnings then being sent home is usual).
- What is the banning procedure? Are young people escorted from the building? By how many members of staff? Who will ring the parents to explain the ban and procedure? Is a ban followed by a letter to parents?
- What happens before young people are readmitted?

→ **Make sure all young people understand the ground rules and consequences**
- Make sure they are clearly displayed on posters around the building.
- Go through them with each young person and get them to sign a copy (for you to keep) and have a copy for themselves.

Preparation – Staff

→ **Make sure that all staff understand the ground rules and consequences**
- This needs discussion and agreement as assumptions lead to frustration and confusion.
- Staff consistency is essential, as inconsistency leads to resentment and boundary pushing from young people.
- Ensure that processes are understood, as well as outcomes.

Implementation

→ **Is zero-tolerance appropriate?**
- It's a good way to implement new rules and change cultures.
- Is it more appropriate to use distraction techniques (interesting programme, vigilance for trouble spots) or both?

→ **Staff co-ordination**
- A system (usually a log behind the coffee bar) needs to be in place so that staff know who has been warned for what.
- For situations that could turn aggressive, a minimum of two staff should speak to the young people. Remember the audience factor – a staff member needs to remove a potential 'audience' of young people as soon as possible, or young people need to be

© Somerset Youth and Community Service 2013

taken to a private part of the building.

- If things get out of hand, ringing the police/parents is always an option. Build a relationship with the local police/PCSO and encourage them to drop in for a coffee regularly.

→ **Repeat unacceptable behaviour**
- Is it acceptable to ban a young person for unacceptable behaviour?
- Other young people's needs must be considered and if a young person's behaviour makes the club unsafe for others, an immediate ban is appropriate.
- If a young person repeatedly behaves badly the bans need to be for longer periods. It is not acceptable to ban a young person for ever (unless in exceptional circumstances) but bans of a term are useful to get the point across.

Sample ground rules and consequences:

- Respect the building
- Respect each other
- Respect the staff and do as they ask you to
- Respect the equipment
- If you're not happy with anything that is happening, talk to staff – unless staff know, they can't help!
- Make new members welcome
- Let staff know what activities you'd like to do at youth club
- Be a good role model to other young people
- Consider our neighbours and behave politely to them
- Smoke out the back of the building
- Illegal drugs and alcohol are not allowed
- If someone is being bullied or upset, let staff know

If you don't keep to the ground rules, there are consequences! These are:

- If you break a ground rule, you will usually get a warning, but if your behaviour is very bad, you could be sent home immediately and your parents will be told.
- You only get two warnings per evening, then you'll be sent home and your parents will be told.
- If your behaviour is very bad, you can be banned from the youth club.

Sample banning and re-admittance procedure:

- A young person is asked to leave and escorted out, being told why they are being banned.
- They are also told that they need to come to youth club 15 minutes early next week to talk to the worker in charge who will decide if they can be re-admitted.
- Parents are telephoned or written to as soon as possible, explaining the ban, asking them to support the youth worker by discussing the behaviour with their son/daughter.
- During this conversation with the worker in charge (with another member of staff present or near by), the worker tries to ensure they understand why they were banned and they must make a commitment to behaving differently.
- *If the worker is not convinced of the young person's sincerity, do not let them back in.*
- If they are readmitted, it is usual to have a one (or no) warning rule before a further ban, for the first couple of weeks.

Appendix 56

Monitoring Visit Sheet

Visit by:	

Date & time visit made:		Length of visit:	

Date report written:	

1. **Staffing** – please enter the names of staff:	

2. Number of young people attending:

Male	Under 13		13-16		17-19		Over 19	
Female	Under 13		13-19		17-19		Over 19	

Black or Minority Ethnic young people		Young people with a Disability	

		Staff No.		Young People No.
Staff to young people ratio of session attended:			:	
	=	1	:	

{Divide number of young people by number of adults present.}

3. Quality of Environment:

Tick the boxes and note your reasons for your judgement

Red		Amber		Green	

Questions to consider:	Notes:

• Does the club look welcoming and friendly? • Is it warm and well lit? • Is it clean and tidy?	

4. Accessibility and Health & Safety:

Tick the boxes and note your reasons for your judgement:

Red		Amber		Green	

Questions to consider:	Notes:
• Can young people with disabilities use the club? • Are there any damaged equipment or fixtures? • Are risk assessments being used? • Has the club done a fire drill in the last term? • Do young people feel safe?	

5. Equality and Diversity:

Tick the boxes and note your reasons for your judgement:

Red		Amber		Green	

Questions to consider:	Notes:
• Are all young people treated fairly? • Is there a bullying policy and do young people know about it? • Are all different sorts of young people encouraged to use the club?	

6. Young People's Participation:

Tick the boxes and note your reasons for your judgement:

Red		Amber		Green	

Questions to consider:	Notes:
<ul><li>Are young people joining in the activities?</li><li>Do young people help to plan the programme?</li><li>Do young people help out? How?</li><li>Are young people listened to by staff?</li><li>Is there a young people's management group?</li></ul>	

7. Quality of advice and information available to young people:

Tick the boxes and note your reasons for your judgement:

Red		Amber		Green	

Questions to consider:	Notes:
<ul><li>Are posters and leaflets up to date and well displayed?</li><li>Do young people know what information/advice is on offer?</li><li>Do young people think the staff are well informed and easy to talk to?</li><li>Do young people feel they have learned anything from attending youth club?</li></ul>	

8. Quality of Delivery:

Tick the boxes and note your reasons for your judgement:

Red		Amber		Green	

Questions to consider:	Notes:
• Is the behaviour good? • Are ground rules and programmes clearly displayed? • What do young people think of the staff, the programme and the youth club overall? • Do young people feel they have achieved anything from attending youth club?	

Comments and suggestions for improvement:

Programme Poster Sample

Ages
13 - 16

Mondays 7:00pm to 9:30pm
@ the Village Hall on the rec

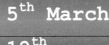

5th March	Healthy Snacks/Film Night
12th March	Team Games/Pizza Making/ Smoking Quiz
19th March	Dance with Dixon/Food Bingo
26th March	Gameshow Night
2nd April	Fitness Night/UniHoc
9th April	Youth Parish Council/ Jewellery Making
16th April	Decks Out/DJ Night
23rd April	Film & Pizza Night

For more information:
Contact Lilith Brown on 01900 000000
www.kittsvilleyouth.co.uk

Sample Session Recording Sheet

Staff:			Date:	Times:
			Visitors:	

Aim of this session and activities provided:

Attendances this session						Income	£	p
	U13	13-15	16-19	20+	Grand Total	Subs		
Male						Tuck/Coffee Bar		
Female						Other (trips etc.)		
Totals						TOTAL		

Reflections on the session: Was the aim of the session achieved? How? What happened? How do you feel about it? What might you have done differently?

Actions for Future: Information to be shared: what and with whom/building/equipment.

Completed by:	See note in incident file:

Sample Signing-in Sheet

Date	Name	Age	Subs paid?	See note in incident file

	U13	13-15	16-19	20+	GRAND TOTALS	Subs Total
Male						
Female						£
Totals						

Sample Tuck Sheet

Date:

Item	Price	Sold	Total
Curly Wurly	*50p*	ЛН1	*£2.50*
Fredo Frog	*10p*	ЛН1 ИН1 II	*£1.20*
Need to re-order:		**Total Tuck:**	*£3.70*

Useful websites

Whilst this information was accurate when it was collated, things change very quickly on the internet so this may not be the case now. Whilst all links have been included in good faith, SCC cannot be held responsible for any content on these sites.

This icon indicates the website has information or downloads which may be useful resources for your club.

Local

Children & Young People's Partnership in Somerset (CHYPPS)	www.chypps.org.uk	
CHYPPS is a member charity that delivers support to organisations in the voluntary sector working with children and young people up to age 25.		
Maze Advocacy	www.mazeadvocacy.net	
Maze helps young people aged 6-19 in Somerset to get their views heard on issues affecting their emotional or mental wellbeing. The service is free, independent and confidential. Contains resources aimed at helping individual young people to sort out their lives.		
Mendip District Council	www.mendip.gov.uk	
SCC Youth & Community Service	www.somersetyouth.co.uk	
Dedicated website for the Somerset County Council Youth & Community Service. The site provides a wide range of information about youth services in Somerset.		
Sedgemoor District Council	www.sedgemoor.gov.uk	
Somerset C&SH	www.somersetcsh.co.uk	
C&SH tell you where to find information and support about many aspects of sexual health including contraception, unplanned pregnancy and treatment for sexually transmitted infections. It also has some good information about taking care of yourself.		
Somerset County Council	www.somerset.gov.uk	
SCC's mission is to provide excellent services that are accessible, responsive and sustainable to ensure Somerset is a healthy and vibrant place to live, work and visit.		
Somerset Rural Youth Project (SRYP)	www.sryp.org.uk	
SRYP is a voluntary youth work charity supporting young people aged 11-25 in rural Somerset in a range of social, economic, educational and recreational opportunities. Contains resources offering instructions for activities and games for youth clubs.		
South Somerset District Council	www.southsomerset.gov.uk	

© Somerset Youth and Community Service 2013

Taunton Deane Borough Council	www.tauntondeane.gov.uk
West Somerset District Council	www.westsomersetonline.gov.uk

National

Action for Children	www.actionforchildren.org.uk	
Action for Children supports and speaks out for the UK's most vulnerable and neglected children and young people, for as long as it takes to make a difference in their lives.		
Amnesty International	www.amnesty.org.uk	
Amnesty is a campaigning organisation. The organisation's purpose is to protect people wherever justice, fairness, freedom and truth are denied. Contains resources linked to Amnesty campaigns.		
Association for Young People's Health	www.youngpeopleshealth.org.uk	
AYPH is a thriving multi-disciplinary membership organisation, working to support professionals in the field of young people's health. Contains resources to guide you through tackling health issues with young people.		
Brook	www.brook.org.uk	
Brook is the only national voluntary sector provider of free and confidential sexual health advice and services specifically for young people under 25. Contains resources such as information leaflets, games and posters.		
Businessballs	www.businessballs.com	
Businessballs is a free ethical learning and development resource for people and organizations. The site features a wealth of resources, including lots of games and quizzes.		
Catch 22	www.catch-22.org.uk	
Catch 22 help young people develop the confidence and skills to find solutions that are right for them – whether it's getting back into school or training, choosing to stay out of trouble, finding a safe place to live or helping them to live independently after leaving care or custody.		
Centre Point	www.centrepoint.org.uk	
Through their approach to supporting homeless young people, collaborating with others and influencing government policy, Centre Point aim to achieve their vision of ending youth homelessness.		
Child-Safe	www.child-safe.org.uk	
Child-Safe is the only child protection charity that aims to safeguard and prevent the abuse of children and young people away from home, particularly in the global youth travel sector. You can order a number of resources from Child-Safe, but charges are payable.		

Childnet International	www.childnet-int.org	

Childnet International is a non-profit organisation working with others to "help make the internet a great and safe place for children". Contains lots of downloadable resources to help young people learn how to stay safe.

Children & Young People's Mental Heath Coalition	www.cypmhc.org.uk	

CYPMHC are a coalition of 14 charities with a growing base of supporters passionate about the wellbeing of the UK's children and young people.

Citizen's Advice Bureau	www.adviceguide.org.uk	

The website provides people with round-the-clock access to CAB information on their rights – including benefits, housing and employment, and on debt, consumer and legal issues. Contains many downloadable fact sheets giving advice and information about rights, many of which would be useful for young people.

Clubs for Young People	www.clubsforyoungpeople.org.uk	

This is a network made up of over 3,000 voluntary youth clubs, youth groups and projects across the UK, helping close to half a million young people each year.

DirectGov	www.direct.gov.uk/en/YoungPeople	

DirectGov is the home for government information and services. The 'Young People' section contains a wealth of information on all aspects of life for young people.

Drinkaware	www.drinkaware.co.uk	

Drinkaware aims to change the UK's drinking habits for the better by promoting responsible drinking and finding innovative ways to challenge the national drinking culture to help reduce alcohol misuse and minimise alcohol-related harm. Resources include downloadable fact sheets and online tools.

Duke of Edinburgh's Award	www.dofe.org	

Leading youth charity the D of E gives all young people the chance to develop skills for work and life, fulfil their potential and have a brighter future.

Equality & Human Rights Commission	www.equalityhumanrights.com	

The commission promotes and monitors human rights: protect, enforce and promote equality across the nine 'protected' grounds – age, disability, gender, race, religion and belief, pregnancy and maternity, marriage and civil partnership, sexual orientation and gender reassignment. Resources include information about young people's rights, although these are not young people friendly!

Family Planning Association	www.fpa.org.uk	

The FPA is a leading sexual health charity. They give straightforward information, advice and support on sexual health, sex and relationships to everyone in the UK. Resources include a wide range of downloadable information leaflets, other resources can be ordered at a cost.

FRANK	www.talktofrank.com	

FRANK helps you find out everything you might want to know about drugs (and some stuff you don't). For friendly, confidential advice, "Talk to FRANK". Contains lots of young people friendly information and downloads.

HIV Aware	www.hivaware.org.uk	

Provided by National AIDS Trust (NAT), the UK's leading charity dedicated to transforming society's response to HIV. They provide fresh thinking, expertise and practical resources. They champion the rights of people living with HIV and campaign for change. Contains downloadable information leaflets and posters.

Joseph Rowntree Foundation	www.jrf.org.uk	

JRF wants lasting change for people and places in poverty, communities where everyone can thrive and a more equal society. Now and for future generations. Resources include a wide range of publications, which can be download free of charge. However, they are aimed at professionals and are not young people friendly!

Mental Health Foundation	www.mentalhealth.org.uk	

The foundation is a leading UK mental health research, policy and service improvement charity. Resources include a range of downloadable publications, but they are aimed at adults.

National Council for Voluntary Youth Services	www.ncvys.org.uk	

The National Council for Voluntary Youth Services is a network of national organisations and regional and local networks that work to build thriving communities and sustainable networks that help all young people achieve their potential. Resources include lots of information and publications for professionals and young people.

National Youth Agency	www.nya.org.uk	

NYA works in partnership with a wide range of public, private and voluntary sector organisations to support and improve services for young people. Contains a range of useful resources, but they are charged for.

National Health Services (NHS)	www.nhs.uk	

NHS Choices is the online 'front door' to the NHS. It is the country's biggest health website and gives all the information you need to make choices about your health. Lots of downloadable information, which would be really useful for young people.

No Smoking Day	www.nosmokingday.org.uk	

Established in 1983, No Smoking Day works to support smokers who want to quit. Contains free downloadable fact sheets for each region of the UK.

Prince's Trust	www.princes-trust.org.uk	

The Prince's Trust gives practical and financial support, developing key workplace skills such as confidence and motivation. They work with 13 to 30-year-olds who have struggled at school, have been in care, are long-term unemployed or have been in trouble with the law.

Raleigh International	www.raleighinternational.org	
Raleigh International offers a number of different programmes for individuals and groups of all nationalities and backgrounds. Whatever your situation, we have a programme for you.		
Samaritans	www.samaritans.org	
Samaritans is a confidential emotional support service for anyone in the UK and Ireland.		
Shelter	www.shelter.org.uk	
Shelter works to alleviate the distress caused by homelessness and bad housing, by giving advice, information and advocacy to people in housing need, and by campaigning for lasting political change to end the housing crisis for good.		
Talented Young People	www.talentedyoungpeople.com	
A free interactive resource for young people aged 13-24 who have dreams to fulfil but need a helping hand on the way. The website is a one stop shop where they can get advice, ideas, talk to experts, talk to other talented young people and promote themselves. Resources include a range of downloadable articles offering advice for young people.		
Think You Know	www.thinkuknow.co.uk	
Think You Know is provided by the Child Exploitation and Online Protection (CEOP) Centre. Find the latest information on the sites you like to visit, mobiles and new technology.		
UK Youth – Positive About Youth	www.ukyouth.org	
UK Youth is a charity at the heart of a national network of organisations dedicated to supporting young people to realise their potential by developing and promoting non-formal learning opportunities. Resources include downloadable programme materials including games and activities.		
UK Youth Parliament	www.ukyouthparliament.org.uk	
Run by young people, the UK Youth Parliament provides opportunities for 11-18 year-olds to use their voice in creative ways to bring about social change.		
Wise Kids	www.wisekids.org.uk	
WISE KIDS is a not-for-profit company that provides innovative training programmes and consultancy in new media, internet & mobile technologies, internet proficiency, literacy & safety. Contains a wide range of resources for use with young people.		
Young Minds	www.youngminds.org.uk	
YoungMinds is a charity committed to improving the emotional wellbeing and mental health of children and young people. They campaign, research and influence policy and practice.		

International

World Youth Alliance	www.wya.net

The World Youth Alliance is a global coalition of young people promoting the dignity of the person and building solidarity among developed and developing nations.

World Health Organisation	www.who.int

WHO is the directing and coordinating authority for health within the United Nations. It is responsible for providing leadership on global health matters, shaping the health research agenda, setting norms and standards, articulating evidence-based policy options, providing technical support to countries and monitoring and assessing health trends.

United Nations	www.un.org/en

The United Nations is an international organisation founded in 1945 after the Second World War by 51 countries committed to maintaining international peace and security, developing friendly relations among nations and promoting social progress, better living standards and human rights.

Questionnaire Sample

Your Club, Your Views...

1. What do you think of the activities on offer at youth club?

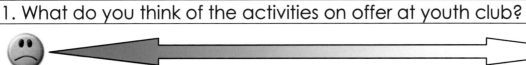

Why do you think this?

2. Circle three words that describe what you think of the staff...

Friendly   Boring   Not interested   Unfriendly   Unfair
Annoying   Interesting   Bullying   Encouraging
Fun!   Helpful   Cool!   Fair   Creepy   Understanding

3. What have you learnt at youth club?

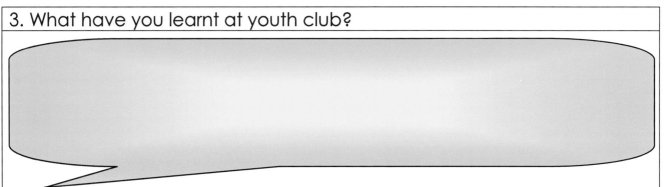

4. Do your views get listened too?	Yes	No

How? Or why not?

5. What do you think of the building?

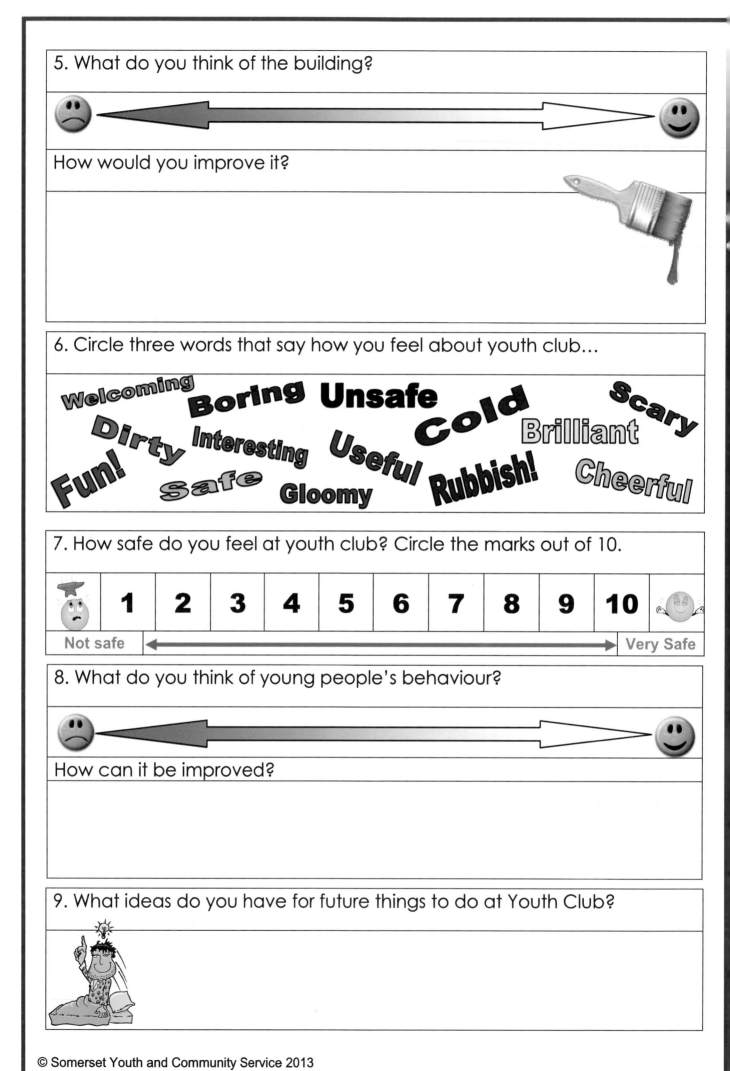

How would you improve it?

6. Circle three words that say how you feel about youth club...

Welcoming Boring Unsafe Cold Scary
Dirty Interesting Useful Brilliant
Fun! Safe Gloomy Rubbish! Cheerful

7. How safe do you feel at youth club? Circle the marks out of 10.

	1	2	3	4	5	6	7	8	9	10	

Not safe ←→ Very Safe

8. What do you think of young people's behaviour?

How can it be improved?

9. What ideas do you have for future things to do at Youth Club?